Social Responsibility

Dialogue Books
Published by the Krishnamurti Foundation of America

Social Responsibility
The Mirror of Relationship: Love, Sex, and Chastity

Study Books (series editor Albion W. Patterson)
Published by the Krishnamurti Foundation of America

Action
Choiceless Awareness
The Individual and Society: The Bondage of Conditioning

Theme Books (series editor Mary Cadogan)
Published by Harper & Row, San Francisco

On Freedom
On God
On Living and Dying
On Nature and the Environment
On Relationship
On Right Livelihood

SOCIAL RESPONSIBILITY

A Selection of Passages

For The Study of The Teachings of

J. Krishnamurti

Krishnamurti Foundation of America
P.O. Box 1560, Ojai, California 93024

SOCIAL RESPONSIBILITY
*A Selection of Passages For The Study of The Teachings of
J. Krishnamurti*

All our problems are really individual problems because the individual is society. There is no society without the individual, and as long as the individual does not totally understand himself, his conscious as well as his unconscious self, whatever reforms he may devise, whatever gods he may invent, whatever truths he may seek will have very little significance. So the individual problem is the world problem, which is fairly obvious; and the world problem can come to an end only when the individual understands himself, the activities of his own mind, the workings of his own consciousness. Then there is a possibility of creating a different world, a world in which there are no nationalities, no frontiers of belief, no political or religious dogmas.

Collected Works, vol. IX, pp. 135-6
Sydney, Australia, November 9, 1955

Only a profound inward revolution which alters all our values can create a different environment, an intelligent social structure, and such a revolution can be brought about only by you and me. No new order will arise until we individually break down our own psychological barriers and are free.

Education and the Significance of Life, p. 52

Contents

x

I.   Introduction: "What Can I Do?"

I think we ought to ask fundamental questions of ourselves and not await the answers from others. These fundamental questions must be answered by each one of us and we must not depend on theoreticians, however clever, erudite, scholarly or experienced. For the world is in terrible confusion, mounting sorrow and we are responsible for this; each human being throughout the world is responsible for this frightening confusion. Apparently we depend for explanations on others and we are satisfied with these explanations; but all explanations are naturally verbal and therefore of no great importance. Any description, any explanation of the actual state of the world is useless, it has no meaning; but most of us are satisfied by words, intellectual explanations which have been woven beautifully, or very subtly. It seems to me that we must be beyond all these explanations, whether they are offered by the churches, by the Communists, or by any group of people who are asserting themselves.

What is very important is to ask ourselves these fundamental questions, and to be utterly responsible in finding not only the answer, but, in the very answering of these questions, to *act.* Because with us action is not part of the question and its answer. Surely in the fact of asking these fundamental questions and in discovering the answers for ourselves, that very discovery must be expressed in action. The questioning, the answering and the action are simultaneous and not separate. Because when they are separate then everything is broken up into departments, categories; and out of that division arise prejudices, conflicts, opinions and judgments. Whereas, it seems to me, if we could really ask, in the very asking we would discover the understanding of question and action; they are not separate. And during these talks, I hope we shall be able not only to ask ourselves these questions but also to understand them, not intellectually or verbally, but with our hearts and with our minds. In this process of understanding, action takes place.

One of the fundamental questions consists in man's relationship to reality. That reality has been expressed in different ways: in the East in one way and in the West in another. If we do not discover for ourselves what that relationship is, independently of the theoreticians and the theologians and the priests, we are incapable of discovering what relationship with reality is. That reality may be named as God—and the name is really of very little importance—because the name, the word, the symbol, is never the actual, and to be caught in symbols and words seems utterly foolish—and yet we are so caught, Christians in one way, Hindus, Muslims and others in other ways—and words and symbols have become extraordinarily significant. But the symbol, the word, is never the actual, the real thing. So in asking the question, as to what is the true relationship of man to reality, one must be free of the word with all its associations, with all its prejudices and conditions. If we do not find that relationship, then life has really very little meaning; then our confusion, our misery is bound to grow, and life will become more and more intolerable, superficial, meaningless. One must be extraordinarily serious to find out if there is such a reality, or if there is not, and what is man's relationship to it.

Now we want to find out first if there is something immeasurable (beyond all reach of thought, above all measurement) a thing that cannot possibly be touched by words, that has no symbol. Is it possible, first of all—not mystically, not romantically or emotionally, but actually—to discoverer, or to come upon this extraordinary state? The ancients and some who throughout the world have perhaps come upon it unknowingly, have said 'there is something'. Serious-minded men for millions of years have attempted to find that. Those who are casual, flippant, have their own reward, their own way of life, but there is always a small minority who are really earnest, who come upon this endless, measureless thing. To understand it, one must obviously be free of all dogma, of all belief, of all the traditional impediments which condition the mind, which are merely inventions of thought. We are human beings, suffering, lonely, confused, in great sorrow, whether we call ourselves Communists or Socialists or anything else—we are human beings. But apparently the important thing for us is the label, French, German or any other. It is important to be free from all this because you need freedom, not merely verbally but actually. It is only in freedom that you can discover what is the real, not through beliefs and dogmas.

So, if one is really earnest in the sense that one is willing to go to the very end, then there must be this freedom—freedom from all nationalities, freedom from all dogma, ritual, beliefs. And apparently this is one of the most difficult things to do. You find in India people who have thought a great deal about these matters and yet they remain soaked in Hindu tradition. In the West they are immersed in the Catholic, Protestant, or Communist dogmas and so they cannot possibly break through. And if one is to have a different kind of life, a life at a different dimension, one must not only be free consciously from all this, but also deep down in the very roots of one's being. Then only is one capable of really looking, seeing. Because to find reality the mind must be sane, healthy, highly intelligent, which means highly sensitive.

What is important is to have a mind that has never been tortured, never been forced into a certain pattern. As one observes throughout the world, religions have maintained that to find reality you must torture yourself, you must deny everything, every sensuous pleasure, you must discipline yourself until your whole mind is shaped according to a pattern which has been established; so that the mind, at the end, has lost the pliability, the quickness, the sensitivity, the beauty of movement. What is necessary is a mind that is untortured, a mind that is very clear. And such a mind is not possible if it has any kind of prejudice. You know one of the most difficult things is to observe, to look: to look at anything without the image of that thing, to look at a cloud without the previous associations with regard to that cloud, to see a flower without the image, the memories, the associations, concerning that flower. Because these associations, these images and memories, create distance between the observer and the observed. And in that distance, the division between the seer and the thing seen, in that division the whole conflict of man exists. It is necessary to see without the image, so that the space between the observer and the thing observed is simply not there. When that space exists then there is conflict, which we shall go into, if we have time, this evening. So the art of seeing is very important. As we said, if we see ourselves with the images which we have built about ourselves, then there is conflict between the image and the fact. And all our life is this conflict between what is and what should be.

Now, please, do not merely listen to these words, phrases and expressions, but observe as we go along, not analytically, but actually observe the process of your own mind; see how it is working, how it is looking at itself. Then you will be actually listening, not trying to translate what you hear according to your prejudices and conditioning. Because the world is in such a frightful state, there is such catastrophe and misery that we must live a different kind of life, there must be fundamental revolution in our way of living. Man has apparently chosen war, conflict, as the way of life and there is a revolt among the young against all this. But unfortunately such a revolt has very little meaning unless one has found for oneself the basic answers to the fundamental questions of life.

One of the primary questions is: what is this thing called reality? Can you and I, living our daily lives (not retiring into a monastery, or becoming disciples of some guru, or running off to some strange academy in India) can we find this reality for ourselves? And we must—not through prayers, nor imitation, nor following somebody, but through becoming aware of our own conditioning, seeing it actually not theoretically, seeing as you would see a flower, a cloud and seeing without separation. I do not know if you have ever tried to look at anything, to look, for example, at your own wife or husband; to look without the image that you or he has built through a relationship of many years, of many irritations, pleasures, angers, to look at each other without the image. I do not know if you have ever tried this; but, if you have, you will have found how extraordinarily difficult it is to be free of images. It is these images which are expected to enter into relationship, not human beings. You have an image about me, and I have an image about you, and the relationship is between these two images with their symbols, associations and memories.

There will be division as long as there is the image which engenders the whole structure of conflict. So one must learn the art of looking, not only at the clouds and the flowers, at the movement of a tree in the wind, but actually looking at ourselves as we are, not saying, 'It is ugly', 'It is beautiful, or 'Is that all?'—all the verbal assertions that one has with regard to oneself. When we can look at ourselves clearly, without the image, then perhaps we shall be able to discover what is true for ourselves. And that truth is not in the realm of thought but of direct perception, in which there is no separation between the observer and the observed. One of the fundamental questions is man's relationship to the ultimate, to the nameless, to what is beyond all words.

Then there is the fundamental question of man's relationship to man. This relationship is society, the society which we have created through our envy, greed, hatred, brutality, competition and violence. Our chosen relationship to society, based on a life of battle, of wars, of conflict, of violence, of aggression, has gone on for thousands of years and has become our daily life, in the office, at home, in the factory, in churches. We have invented a morality out of this conflict, but it is no morality at all, it is a morality of respectability, which has no meaning whatsoever. You go to church and love your neighbour there and in the office you destroy him.

When there are nationalistic differences based on ideas, opinions, prejudices, a society in which there is terrible injustice, inequality— we all know this, we are terribly aware of all this—aware of the war that is going on, of the action of the politicians and the economists trying to bring order out of disorder—we are aware of this. And we say, 'What can we do?' We are aware that we have chosen a way of life that leads ultimately to the field of murder. We have probably asked this, if we are at all serious, a thousand times but we say 'I, as a human being, can't do anything. What can I do faced with this colossal machine?'

When one puts a question to oneself such as 'What can I do?'— I think one is putting the wrong question. To that there is no answer. If you do answer it then you will form an organization, belong to something, commit yourself to a particular course of political, economic, social action; and you are back again in the same old circle in your particular organization with its presidents, secretaries, money, its own little group, against all other groups. We are caught in this. 'What can I do?' is a totally wrong question— you can't do a thing when you put the question that way. But you can, when you *actually see* (as you see the microphone and the speaker sitting here) actually see that each one of us is responsible for the war that is going on in the Far East, and that it is not the Americans, nor the Vietnamese, nor the Communists, but you and I who are responsible, actually, desperately responsible for what is going on in the world, not only there but everywhere. We are responsible for the politicians, whom we have brought into being, responsible for the army which is trained to kill, responsible for all our actions, conscious or unconscious.

But you say, 'We don't want to be responsible', we are frightened to say 'I am responsible for this whole monumental mess'. But if you actually, with your heart, feel this thing, then you will act, then you will find that you are totally outside society. You may have a few clothes, go about in a car and all the rest of it, but in order to be truly moral you will have to be psychologically, inwardly, completely out of society, which is to deny all morality. If you accept the present structure of morality then you are actually immoral. There is corruption, society is going down-hill. You know about the riots in America—and about what is happening in the Near East and worse in the Far East and in India where there is immense starvation. Each country feels that it has to solve the problems for itself while politicians throughout the world are playing a game with starvation, with murder, because we have divided the world into nationalities, into sovereign governments, with different flags. And to bring about order, the concern of every human being must be the unity of man. That means a government which is not divided into French, German and all the other nationalities.

Don't you often wonder why politicians exist at all? A government can be run by computers, impersonal, non-ambitious, not people who are seeking their own personal glory in the name of their nation; then we might have a sane government! But you see, unfortunately, human beings are not sane, they want to live in this immense mess. And you and I are responsible for it. Don't, please, merely agree, or shake your head in assent; you have to do something about it. The doing *is* the seeing, the listening. You know when you see a danger you act, there is no hesitation, there is no argument, there is no personal opinion, there is immediate action. But you don't see the immense danger of what is going on in the world around you, in the educational system, the business world, the religious world—you don't see the danger of all that. But to see the danger of it is to act. When you see something actually then there is no conflict, there is immediate movement away from the thing, without resistance, without conflict.

To look at social injustice, social misery, social morality and culture in the midst of which organized religions exist, and to deny their validity psychologically, is to become extraordinarily moral. Because after all morality is order; virtue is complete order. And that can only come into being when you deny disorder, the disorder in which we live, the disorder of conflict, of fear in which each individual is seeking personal security. I do not know if you have ever considered the question of security. You know we find security in commitment; in being committed to something there is a great feeling of security, in being a Communist, in being a Frenchman, or an Englishman, or anything else. That commitment gives us security. If you have committed yourself to a course of action, that commitment gives a great deal of surety, assurance, certainty. But that commitment always breeds disorder, and this is what is actually taking place. I am a Communist and you are not—whatever you are. We are committed to ideas, to theories, to slogans and so we divide, as you are this and I am that. Whereas if we are involved, not committed, involved in the whole movement of life then there is no division; then we are human beings in sorrow, not a Frenchman in sorrow, not a Catholic in sorrow, but human beings who are guilty, anxious, in agony, lonely, bored with the routine of life. If you are involved in it, then we'll find a way out of it together. But we like to be committed, we like to be separately secure, not only nationalistically, communally, but also individually. And in this commitment there is isolation. When the mind is isolated it is not sane.

We may all know this verbally, because most people have read a great deal about all this, but unfortunately what they have read does not constitute a discovery of themselves, it is not their own discovery, their own understanding. For that, one must investigate, look at oneself without any criteria, look at oneself with choiceless awareness so as to see exactly what one is, not what one should be. And when you see exactly what you are then there is no conflict.

Also there is the question of love and death. Again the thing which we call love has really lost its meaning. When one says, 'I love you' there is an abundance of pleasure in this. So one has to find out for oneself if love is pleasure; this doesn't mean one must deny pleasure to find love; but when love is hedged about with greed, with jealousy, hate, envy, as it is with most of us—is this love? When love is divided as the divine and ordinary, sensuous love—is it love? Or is not love something that is not touched by pleasure?

One has to go into this question of what pleasure is. Why is everything based on pleasure? The search for what you call 'God' is based on pleasure. One derives pleasure from having possessions, prestige, position, power, domination. But without love, do what you will, be as clever as you like, you will solve nothing. Whatever you do you will create more misery for yourself and for another.

Then we come again to this extraordinary question of the nature of death. That must be answered, neither with fear, nor by escaping from that absolute fact, nor by belief, nor hope. There is an answer, the right answer, but to find the right answer one has to put the right question. But you cannot possibly put the right question if you are merely seeking a way out of it, if the question is born of fear, of despair and of loneliness. Then if you do put the right question with regard to reality, with regard to man's relationship to man, and what that thing called love is, and also this immense question of death, then out of the right question will come the right answer. From that answer comes right action. Right action is in the answer itself. And we are responsible. Don't fool yourself by saying 'What can I do? What can I, an individual, living a shoddy little life, with all its confusion and ignorance, what can I do?' Ignorance exists only when you don't know yourself. Self-knowing is wisdom. You may be ignorant of all the books in the world (and I hope you are), of all the latest theories, but that is not ignorance. Not knowing oneself deeply, profoundly, is ignorance; and you cannot know yourself if you cannot look at yourself, see yourself actually as you are, without any distortion, without any wish to change. Then what you see is transformed because the distance between the observer and the observed is removed and hence there is no conflict.

Talks in Europe 1968, pp. 47-56
Paris, April 16, 1968

II.   What Is Your Responsibility To Society?

It must be fairly obvious to each one of us when we look at the world...that there must be some kind of fundamental revolution. I am using that word to convey, not a superficial, patchwork reformation, nor a revolution instigated as a calculated risk according to a particular pattern of thought, but the revolution that can come about only at the highest level, when we begin to understand the whole significance of the mind. Without understanding this fundamental issue, it seems to me that any reformation at any level, however beneficial temporarily, is bound to lead to further misery and chaos.

Seeing this extraordinarily complex pattern of wealth and poverty, of sovereign governments, of armies and the latest instruments of mass destruction, one asks oneself what is going to come out of all this chaos, and where it is all going to lead. What is the answer? If one is at all serious, I think one must have asked oneself this question. How are we, as individuals and as groups, to tackle this problem? Being confused, most of us turn to some kind of pattern, religious or social; we look to some leader to guide us out of this chaos, or we insist on returning to the ancient traditions. We say, "Let us go back to what the *rishis* have taught us, which is all in the Upanishads, in the Gita; let us have more prayers, more rituals, more gurus, more Masters." This is actually what is happening, is it not?

Now, looking at this whole chaotic picture—not philosophically, not merely as an observer watching the events go by, but as one whose sympathies are stirred and who has a germ of compassion, which I am sure most of us have—how do you respond to it all?

What is your responsibility to society? Or are you merely caught in the wheels of society, following the traditional pattern set by a particular culture, Western or Eastern, and are therefore blind to the whole issue? And if you do open your eyes, are you merely concerned with social reform, political action, economic adjustment? Does the solution to this enormously complex problem lie anywhere there, or does it lie in a totally different direction? Is the problem merely economic and social? Or is there chaos and the constant threat of war because most of us are not concerned at all with the deeper issues of life, with the total development of man?

Now, seeing this state of things—of which I am sure you are very much aware unless you are insensitive or are trying to block it off—what is your answer? Please do not answer theoretically, according to the communist, the capitalist, the Hindu, or some other pattern, which is merely an imposition and therefore not true, but instead strip the mind of all its immediate reactions, the so-called educated reactions, and find out what is your reaction as individuals. How would you solve this problem?

If you ask the communist this question, he has a very definite answer, and so has the Catholic or the orthodox Hindu or Moslem, but their answers are obviously conditioned. They have been educated to think along certain lines, narrow or wide, by a society or culture which is not at all concerned with the total development of the mind; and because they are responding from their conditioned thinking, their answers are inevitably in contradiction and must therefore always create enmity, which I think is again fairly obvious. If you are a Hindu, a Christian, or what you will, your response is bound to be according to your conditioned background, the culture in which you have been brought up. The problem is beyond all cultures, beyond any particular pattern, yet we are seeking an answer in terms of a particular pattern, and hence there is mounting confusion, greater misery. So unless there is a fundamental breaking away from all conditioning, a total cleavage, we shall obviously create more chaos, however well-intentioned or so-called religious we may be.

It seems to me that the problem lies at a different level altogether, and in understanding it, I think, we shall bring about an action entirely different from that of the socialistic, the capitalistic, or the communistic pattern. To me, the problem is to understand the ways of the mind because unless one is able to observe and understand the process of thought in oneself, there is no freedom, and hence one cannot go very far. With most of us, the mind is not free; it is consciously or unconsciously tethered to some form of knowledge, to innumerable beliefs, experiences, dogmas; and how can such a mind be capable of discovery, of searching out something new?

To every challenge there must obviously be a new response because today the problem is entirely different from what it was yesterday. Any problem is always new; it is undergoing transformation all the time. Each challenge demands a new response, and there can be no new response if the mind is not free. So freedom is at the beginning, not just at the end. Revolution must begin, surely, not at the social, cultural, or economic level, but at the highest level; and the discovery of the highest level is the problem—the discovery of it, not the acceptance of what is said to be the highest level. I don't know if I am explaining myself clearly on this point. One can be told what is the highest level by some guru, some clever individual, and one can repeat what one has heard, but that process is not discovery; it is merely the acceptance of authority, and most of us accept authority because we are lazy. It has all been thought out, and we merely repeat it like a gramophone record.

Now, I see the necessity of discovery because it is obvious that we have to create a totally different kind of culture—a culture not based on authority but on the discovery by each individual of what is true, and that discovery demands complete freedom. If a mind is held, however long its tether, it can only function within a fixed radius, and therefore it is not free. So what is important is to discover the highest level at which revolution can take place, and that demands great clarity of thought; it demands a good mind—not a phony mind which is repetitive, but a mind that is capable of hard thinking, of reasoning to the end, clearly, logically, sanely. One must have such a mind, and only then is it possible to go beyond.

So revolution, it seems to me, can take place only at the highest level, which must be discovered; and you can discover it only through self-knowledge, not through the knowledge gathered from your ancient books, or from the books of modern analysts. You must discover it in relationship—discover it, and not merely repeat something that you have read or heard. Then you will find that the mind becomes extraordinarily clear. After all, the mind is the only instrument we have. If that mind is clogged, petty, fearful, as most of our minds are, its belief in God, its worship, its search for truth has no meaning at all. It is only the mind that is capable of clear perception, and therefore of being very quiet, that can discover whether there is truth or not, and it is only such a mind that can bring about revolution at the highest level. Only the religious mind is truly revolutionary, and the religious mind is not the mind that repeats, that goes to church or to the temple, that does puja every morning, that follows some kind of guru or worships an idol. Such a mind is not religious; it is really a silly, limited mind; therefore, it can never freely respond to challenge.

This self-knowledge is not to be learned from another. I cannot tell you what it is. But one can see how the mind operates, not just the mind that is active every day, but the totality of the mind, the mind that is conscious as well as hidden. All the many layers of the mind have to be perceived, investigated—which does not mean introspection. Self-analysis does not reveal the totality of the mind because there is always the division between the analyzer and the analyzed. But if you can observe the operation of your own mind without any sense of judgment, evaluation, without condemnation or comparison—just observe it as you would observe a star, dispassionately, quietly, without any sense of anxiety—then you will see that self-knowledge is not a matter of time, that it is not a process of delving into the unconscious to remove all the motives, or to understand the various impulses and compulsions. What creates time is comparison, surely, and because our minds are the result of time, they are always thinking in terms of the 'more', which we call progress.

So, being the result of time, the mind is always thinking in terms of growth, of achievement; and can the mind free itself from the 'more', which is really to dissociate itself completely from society? Society insists on the 'more'. After all, our culture is based on envy and acquisitiveness, is it not? Our acquisitiveness is not only in material things but also in the realm of so-called spirituality, where we want to have more virtue, to be nearer the Master, the guru. So the whole structure of our thinking is based on the 'more', and when one completely understands the demand for the 'more', with all its results, there is surely a complete dissociation from society; and only the individual who is completely dissociated from society can act upon society. The man who puts on a loincloth or a sanyasi's robe, who merely becomes a monk, is not disassociated from society; he is still part of society, only his demand for the 'more' is at another level. He is still conditioned by, and therefore caught within, the limits of a particular culture.

I think this is the real issue, and not how to produce more things and distribute what is produced. The basic problem is that man is not creative; he has not discovered for himself this extraordinary source of creativity which is not an invention of the mind.

Collected Works, vol. IX, pp. 193-6
Madras, India, January 11, 1956

There can be fundamental revolution only when we understand our relationship to the collective

In all our relationships—with people, with nature, with ideas, with things—we seem to create more and more problems. In trying to solve one problem, whether economic, political, social, collective, or individual, we introduce many other problems. We seem somehow to breed more and more conflict and need more and more reform. Obviously, all reform needs further reform, and therefore it is really retrogression. As long as revolution, whether of the left or the right, is merely the continuity of what has been in terms of what shall be, it also is retrogression. There can be fundamental revolution, a constant inward transformation, only when we, as individuals, understand our relationship to the collective. The revolution must begin with each one of us, and not with external, environmental influences. After all, we are the collective; both the conscious and the unconscious in us is the residue of all the political, social, cultural influences of man. Therefore, to bring about a fundamental outward revolution, there must be a radical transformation within each one of us, a transformation which does not depend on environmental change. It must begin with you and me. All great things start on a small scale, all great movements begin with you and me as individuals; and if we wait for collective action, such collective action, if it takes place at all, is destructive and conducive to further misery.

So, revolution must begin with you and me. That revolution, that individual transformation, can take place only when we understand relationship, which is the process of self-knowledge. Without knowing the whole process of my relationship at all the different levels, what I think and what I do has no value at all. What basis have I for thinking if I do not know myself? We are so desirous to act, so eager to do something, to bring some kind of revolution, some kind of amelioration, some change in the world;

but without knowing the process of ourselves both at the periphery and inwardly, we have no basis for action, and what we do is bound to create more misery, more strife. The understanding of oneself does not come through the process of withdrawal from society or through retirement into an ivory tower. If you and I really go into the matter carefully and intelligently, we will see that we can understand ourselves only in relationship and not in isolation. Nobody can live in isolation. To live is to be related. It is only in the mirror of relationship that I understand myself, which means that I must be extraordinarily alert in all my thoughts, feelings, and actions in relationship. This is not a difficult process or a superhuman endeavor; and as with all rivers, while the source is hardly perceptible, the waters gather momentum as they move, as they deepen. In this mad and chaotic world, if you go into this process advisedly, with care, with patience, without condemning, you will see how it begins to gather momentum and that it is not a matter of time.

Collected Works, vol. VI, pp. 37-8
Madras, February 5, 1950

Where does one begin to bring about this fundamental change which is so obviously essential in the social order?

We realize that there must be a fundamental change in our way of thinking, a radical transformation of the human mind and heart, but this extraordinary change cannot be brought about by merely continuing what has been in a modified form. Nor can this radical revolution in the mind be brought about through education as it now exists, for what we now call education is merely the learning of a technique in order to earn a livelihood and conform to the pattern imposed by society.

So, seeing all this, where are we to begin? Where does one begin to bring about this fundamental change which is so obviously essential in the social order? Surely, the individual problem is the world problem. Society is what we have made it. There are those who have, and those who have not, those who know, and those who are ignorant, those who are fulfilling their ambition, and those who are frustrated; there are the various religions, with their ceremonies and dogmatic beliefs, and the ceaseless battle within society, this everlasting competition with each other to achieve, to become. All this is what you and I have created. Social reforms may be brought about through legislation or through tyranny, but unless the individual radically changes, he will always overcome the new pattern to suit his psychological demands—which is again what is happening in the world.

It seems to me very important, then, to understand the total process of individuality, because it is only when the individual changes radically that there can be a fundamental revolution in society. It is always the individual, never the group or the collective, that brings about a radical change in the world, and this again is historically so.

Now, can the individual, that is, you and I, change radically? This transformation of the individual—but not according to a pattern—is what we are concerned with, and to me it is the highest form of education. It is this transformation of the individual that constitutes religion, not the mere acceptance of a dogma, a belief, which is not religion at all. The mind that is conditioned to a particular pattern which it calls religion, whether Hindu, Christian, Buddhist, or what you will, is not a religious mind, however much it may practice all the so-called religious ideals.

Collected Works, vol. IX, p. 226
Madanapalle, India, February 19, 1956

The very structure of society is the structure of yourself

Because this society in which we live, we have created, we are responsible for it—each one of us. It has not come into being because of some fictitious, spiritual forces. It has come about through our greed, through our ambition, through our personal like, and dislike, and enmities, through our frustrations, through our search for pleasure and satisfaction. We have created the religions, the beliefs, the dogmas, out of fear. It is in that society that you live. Either you run away from that society because you cannot understand it, or cannot bring about a change in that society of which you are a part; or you become so completely engrossed in your own particular travail that you lose complete interest in the radical demand of a human mind that says that it must change.

So, existence is relationship, existence is a movement in relationship, and that existence is society. And we cannot possibly go beyond the limits of our mind, of our heart, unless we understand the structure of our own being, which is society. The society is not different from you—you are society. The very structure of society is the structure of yourself. So when you begin to understand yourself, you are then beginning to understand the society in which you live. It is not opposed to society. So a religious man is concerned with the discovery of a new way of life, of living in this world, and bringing about a transformation in the society in which he lives, because by transforming himself, he transforms society. I think this is very important to understand.

Collected Works, vol. XV, p. 50
Bombay, India, February 10, 1965

What you are, the world is, and without your transformation, there can be no transformation of the world

So, the first thing is to realize that the world's problem is the individual's problem; it is your problem and my problem, and the world's process is not separate from the individual process. They are a joint phenomenon, and therefore what you do, what you think, what you feel, is far more important than to introduce legislation or to belong to a particular party or group of people. That is the first truth to be realized, which is obvious. A revolution in the world is essential, but revolution according to a particular pattern of action is not a revolution. A revolution can take place only when you, the individual, understand yourself and therefore create a new process of action. Surely, we need a revolution because everything is going to pieces—social structures are disintegrating, there are wars and more wars. We are standing on the edge of a precipice, and obviously there must be some kind of transformation, for we cannot go on as we are. The left offers a kind of revolution, and the right proposes a modification of the left. But such revolutions are not revolutions; they do not solve the problem because the human entity is much too complex to be understood through a mere formula. And as a constant revolution is necessary, it can only begin with you, with your understanding of yourself. That is a fact, that is the truth, and you cannot avoid it from whatever angle you approach it. After seeing the truth of that, you must establish the intention to study the total process of yourself because, what you are, the world is. If your mind is bureaucratic, you will create a bureaucratic world, a stupid world, a world of red tape; if you are greedy, envious, narrow, nationalistic, you will create a world in which there is nationalism, which destroys human beings, a social structure based on greed, division, property, and so on. So, what you are, the world is, and without your transformation, there can be no transformation of the world. But to study oneself demands extraordinary care, extraordinarily swift pliability, and a mind burdened with the desire for a result can never follow the swift movement of thought. So then, the first difficulty is to see the truth that the individual is responsible, that you are responsible for the whole mess, and when you see your responsibility, to establish the intention to observe and therefore to bring about a radical transformation in yourself.

Collected Works, vol. V, pp. 12-13
Bangalore, India, July 11, 1948

At whatever level you live, there is conflict, not only individual conflict, but also world conflict. The world is you; it is not separate from you. What you are, the world is. There must be a fundamental revolution in your relationship with people, with ideas; there must be a fundamental change, and that change must begin, not outside you, but in your relationships. Therefore, it is essential for a man of peace, for a man of thought, to understand himself, for without self-knowledge his efforts only create further confusion and further misery. Be aware of the total process of yourself. You need no guru, no book, to understand from moment to moment your relationship with all things.

Collected Works, vol. VI, p. 54
Colombo, Sri Lanka, January 1, 1950

Question: You say that fundamentally my mind works in exactly the same way as everyone else's. Why does this make me responsible for the whole world?

What the speaker said was, that wherever you go, throughout the world, human beings suffer, are in conflict, they feel anxiety and uncertainty. Both psychologically and physically there is very little security; there is fear, there is loneliness, despair and depression. This is the common lot of human beings whether they live in China, Japan, India, America, Russia or here—everybody goes through this. It is their life. And as a human being you are the whole world psychologically. You are not separate from the man who is suffering, anxious and lonely, in India or in America. You are the world and the world is you. This is a fact which very few people realize, not a philosophical concept, an idea, but a fact—as when you have a headache. And when one realizes that profoundly, then the question arises: what is my responsibility? We are asking each other this question, please. When you realize that, not verbally but in your blood, that you are no longer an individual—which is a great shock for most people, we think our minds, our problems, our anxieties are all ours, personally—when one sees the truth of this matter, then what is our responsibility? What is our responsibility globally—not only for our family, wife and children—but for the whole of mankind, because we are mankind? We have our illusions, our images of God, our images of heaven, our rituals, exactly like the rest of the world, only with different names, but the pattern is the same.

What is your reaction when you feel that you are humanity? How do you respond to the challenge? How do you meet any challenge? If you meet it from your old individual conditioning, your response will naturally be totally inadequate and fragmentary, it will be rather shoddy. So you have to find out what your response is to this great challenge. Does your mind meet it greatly, or with your fears, your anxieties, the little concerns about yourself?

The responsibility depends upon the response to the challenge. Is it just a flutter, a romantic appeal, or something profound that will transform your whole way of looking at life? Then you are no longer British, American, French. Will you give up all that? Or merely play with the idea that it is a marvellous Utopian concept?

Questions and Answers, pp. 89-90
Brockwood Park, England, September 2, 1980

Question: How can the idea, "You are the world and you are totally responsible for the whole of mankind" be justified on a rational, objective, sane basis?

Krishnamurti: One is not sure it can be rationalized on a sane, objective basis. But we will examine first before we say it can't.

First of all the earth on which we live is our earth—right? It is not the British earth, or the French, German, Russian, Indian, or Chinese earth; it is our earth on which we are all living. That is a fact. But thought has divided it racially, geographically, culturally, economically. That division is causing havoc in the world - obviously. There is no denial of that. That is rational, objective, sane. Right? And we have been saying it is the earth of all human beings living on this earth, not the earth of the isolated, divided communities. It is our earth on which we are all living, though politically, economically we have divided it—for security, for various forms of patriotic, illusory reasons—which eventually brings about war.

Please go into this with me. You may disagree, you may say it is all nonsense, but please listen to it and see if it is not rational, objective, sane.

We have also said that all our human consciousness is similar. On whatever part of the earth we live, we all go through a great deal of suffering, a great deal of pain, great anxiety, uncertainty, fear. And we have occasionally, or perhaps often, pleasure. This is the common ground on which all human beings stand. Right? This is an irrefutable fact. We may try to dodge it, we may try to say it is not, that I am an individual and so on, and so on, but when you look at it objectively, non-personally, not as British, French, and so on, in examining it you will find that our consciousness is like the consciousness of all human beings, psychologically. You may be tall, you may be fair, you may have brown hair, I may be black or white, or pink, or whatever it is, but inwardly, psychologically we are all having a terrible time. We all have a great sense of desperate loneliness. You may have children, a husband, and all the rest of it, but when you are alone you have this feeling that you have no relationship with anything, totally isolated. I am sure most of us have had that feeling. And we are saying this is the common ground on which all humanity stands. And whatever happens in the field of this consciousness we are responsible. That is: if I am violent, I am adding violence to that consciousness which is common to all of us. If I am not violent, I am not adding to it, I am bringing a totally new factor to that consciousness. So I am profoundly responsible either to contribute to that violence, to that confusion, to that terrible division; or as I recognize deeply in my heart, in my blood, in the depths of my being, that I am the rest of the world, I am mankind, I am the world, the world is not separate from me, then I become totally responsible. This is obviously rational, objective, sane. The other is insanity; to call oneself a Hindu, a Buddhist, a Christian and all the rest of it—they are just labels.

So when one has that feeling, that reality, sees the truth that every human being living on this earth is responsible not only for himself, but responsible for everything that is happening, how will one translate that in daily life? How will you translate it if you have that feeling? Not as an intellectual conclusion, as an ideal and so on, then it has no reality. But if the truth is that you are standing on the ground which is common to all mankind, and you feel totally responsible, then what is your action towards society, towards the world in which you are actually living? The world as it is now is full of violence. Only a very, very few people escape from it because they are carefully guarded, protected. Suppose I realize I am totally responsible, what is my action then? Shall I join a group of terrorists? Obviously not. Obviously competitiveness between nations is destroying the world—the most powerful, the less powerful, and the less powerful trying to become more powerful, which is competition. Shall I, realizing that I am the rest of mankind and I am totally responsible, shall I be competitive? Please answer these questions. When I feel responsible for this naturally I cease to be competitive.

Also the world, the religious world as well as the economic world, social world, is based on a hierarchical principle. And shall I also have this hierarchical outlook? Obviously not, because that again is the one who says, "I know", and the other who says, "I do not know". The one who says "I know" is now taking a superior position, economically, socially, religiously and has a status. And if you want that status go after it, but you are contributing to the confusion of the world.

So there are actual, objective, sane actions when you perceive, when you realize in your heart of hearts, in the depth of your being that you are the rest of mankind and that we are all standing on the same ground.

Ojai, California, May 14, 1982

There is no way out except that you become aware of this immense responsibility as a human being

As an individual, it is your responsibility to bring about a tremendous change in the world. It is your responsibility, because you are part of this society, because you are part of this tremendous sorrow of man, this constant effort, struggle, pain, and anxiety. You are responsible. Unless you realize that immense responsibility and come directly in contact with that responsibility and listen to the whole structure, the machinery of that responsibility, do what you will—go to every temple, to every guru, to every Master, to every religious book in the world—your action has no meaning whatsoever, because those are mere escapes from actuality.

So we have to understand this existence, this life, our relationship to society. We have not only to understand our relationship with each other, with society, but to bring about a radical change in that relationship. And that is our responsibility. I do not think we feel this urgency. We look to the politicians, we look to some philosophy, we look to something mysterious that will bring about an alteration within ourselves. There is no way out except that you become aware of this immense responsibility as a human being, and becoming aware of that responsibility, you learn all about it and do not bring all your previous knowledge to learn. And to learn there must be freedom; otherwise, you will repeat the same thing over and over again. You cannot learn ahimsa.

I do not know if you have not noticed that there is so much confusion, misery, and sorrow in the world, and that man—the modern-day man—has not been able to find a way out of it. So he resorts to the past. He thinks he must go back to five thousand or seven thousand years and resuscitate that past to bring about a revival. And again, there is no answer that way. There is no answer through time. Time can make life more happy, more comfortable; but comfort and pleasure are not the absolute answers to life. Nor does the answer lie through some reform. Nor is there a way out through any temple, through any sacred book. I think one has to realize the seriousness of all this, and put away all that nonsense, and come face to face with facts—which is our life, our everyday, brutal, anxious, insecure, cruel life, with its pleasures, with its amusements—and to see if one can bring about, as a human being who has lived for two million years, a radical transformation within oneself, and therefore within the structure of society.

To be aware of this responsibility means great, arduous work. We have to work not only within ourselves but also in our relationship with others. I mean by "work" not the practice of some silly formula, some absurd theory, some fantastic assertions of some philosopher or of some guru or teacher. Those are all too infantile, immature. When we talk about work, we mean by that becoming aware of the responsibility, as a human being living in this world, that he has to work to bring about a change within himself. And if he really changes, if he brings about a mutation within himself, then he will transform society. Society is not transformed through any revolution, economic or social. We have seen this through the French Revolution, the Russian Revolution. The everlasting hope of man—that by altering the outward things, the inward nature of man can be transformed—has never been fulfilled, and it will never be. The outward change, the economic change, which is bound to come to this country which is so poor—that is not going to change man's attitude, the ways of life, his misery, his confusion.

So to bring about a total change of man, man has to become aware of himself—that is, he has to learn about himself anew. Man, according to the recent discoveries of anthropology, has lived for two million years; and man has not found a way out of his misery. He has escaped from it, he has run away from some fanciful illusion. But he has not found it, has not built a society that is totally free; he has not built a society which is not a society of conformity.

You know, if you observe, there are those societies which through necessity cooperate. Through necessity, through compulsion, through an industrial revolution, people must live together; they must cooperate, they must conform, they must follow a pattern. And in that society, as one can observe, there are still conflicts; each man is still against the other because he is ambitious, he is competitive, though he may talk about the love of the neighbor. By force he must cooperate but through that cooperation, through that assertion of loving the neighbor, he is competitive, ruthless, ambitious. Therefore such a pattern of society brings about its own destruction.

Then there is a form of society where there is no civic consciousness at all; each man is out for himself. As you observe in this country, each man is concerned with his family, with his group, with his class, with his particular part of the country, with his linguistic divisions; and he has no civic consciousness. He is not at all conscious of what is happening to his neighbor; he does not care; he is totally indifferent to what happens. But yet, if you observe, his religious books have told him that perhaps he will live the next life, therefore, he must behave; that there is karma: what he does now will matter, how he talks, how he tells things, it does not matter to whom; that behavior is righteousness and if he does not behave now, he pays for it next life—this is the crude form. On that you have been brought up for centuries, and yet, such beliefs, such ideas have no importance through your life because you do not believe. You still carry on as though this is the only life that matters. Because you are competitive, you are ambitious, you destroy your neighbor; you are not at all civic minded socially.

So there are these two forms of society. One form of society is such that the human being that lives in it is made to conform, made to cooperate out of necessity. Thus the human being becomes civic minded: he does not throw things out on the road because he would be punished; there is order. But within that order, within that framework, each man is against the other. In the other form of society, as in this country, there is no framework. Here you have no civic consciousness at all because you do not believe one bit in what you think you are being told.

You have these two forms of society, and each of these societies, inherently within itself, has the seed of its own destruction. So, a religious man is concerned with creating a new society which is neither this nor that, but something entirely different—which is, each human being behaves righteously every minute because he understands his responsibility as a human being. He alone is responsible and no other—how he behaves; what his activities are; whether he is ambitious, cruel, destructive, hating, jealous, competitive; what his fears are. It is only such a mind that can bring about a new society.

And we do need a new society, and that society is not going to be created by anybody except by you. I do not think we feel the immense responsibility of this. That is the first thing that matters. Because that is the foundation, which is righteous behavior, right conduct—not the conduct of a pattern, but the conduct which comes about through learning. If you are all the time learning, that very learning brings about its own righteous action. Therefore it is only the religious mind that can create this new society.

Collected Works, vol. XV, pp. 52, 54
Bombay, February 10, 1965

III.   The Importance of the Individual

Without a radical transformation of the individual, society becomes a burden, an irresponsible continuity in which the individual is merely a cog.

> *Collected Works*, vol. XI, p. 171
> New Delhi, India, February 18, 1959

If you would bring order out of this chaos, where would you begin?

Life is a complex problem, and to understand it there must be patient analysis of the problem and not jumping to a comforting conclusion; there must be a sane detachment to understand the actual, the existing problem. So let us take the journey of understanding. In making this journey do not let us jump to any conclusion and action; we shall act, not based upon any conclusion but upon truth. If we are attached, committed to any form of action, we shall not be capable of understanding the complex process of living; if we are too close to the problem, we are incapable of right observation and comprehension. If we are to understand life, there must be no conclusion, for conclusion puts an end to right thinking. As living is a vast process, any conclusion would be petty and biased. So let us discuss together, if we can, seriously and earnestly, the problem of living and not merely listen superficially to a series of talks; though I may talk, it is your life that is concerned, your joys and pains, your sorrows and strifes.

As every phase of life is interrelated, we must not approach it through any exclusive, specialized path; the merely intellectual or merely the emotional, the psychological or the merely physiological, prevents the understanding of the total process, which is life. In emphasizing the one path, the one phase, we only create conclusions which prevent the understanding of the whole. If we only study or specialize in one corner of the picture, we shall not comprehend the significance of the whole. If you specialize in economics and try to comprehend life from that limited point of view, you will inevitably miss the deeper and wider significance of life and so bring about greater confusion. For the time being put aside your specializations and look at life as a whole. The more we specialize, the more limited, destructive, we shall become. Our human problems are not to be solved by specialists, by experts, the few that can comprehend the entire picture, the whole process of life—they will be the saviors and not the specialists, not the experts.

Life, living and action, is a very complex problem which, if you would understand, must be approached very simply. If you would understand a child, a complex entity, you must not impose upon it your conditioning; you must observe without condemnation. If you see a lovely sunset and you compare it with other sunsets you have seen, then the present sunset has no joy. To understand, there must be a mind that is simple, not an innocent mind, but that which perceives directly, and not translates it according to its conditioning. This is one of our major difficulties in the right approach to the comprehension of life.

What is your relationship to the present degradation and chaos, to the prevailing despair? Perhaps you are not deeply aware of this degradation and despair. Everywhere, here and Europe, we see the utter failure of religion and education, the collapse of systems, either of the left or of the right. What is your relationship to this frightful confusion, to this destructive chaos? If you would bring order out of this chaos, where would you begin? Obviously with yourself, for your relationship with this crisis, with this degradation is direct. Let us not put the blame of this disaster on the few unbalanced leaders or on the systems, for you have created this confusion, and to being order and peace out of it, you must begin with yourself; you must put order in your own house. Do not let us consider the rightness or wrongness of systems and formulas which promise hope; do not let us consider theories nor outer revolutions; we must begin with ourselves, for we, you and I, are responsible for this disaster, for this confusion. Without you there is no world; you are the world, you are the problem. This assertion is not an intellectual formulation but an actual fact. Do not set it aside, which only indicates your desire to escape from it. When you recognize your obvious responsibility for the strife and sorrow, what you think, feel, and do, what you are becomes vitally significant, and because you are unwilling to face it, you look to systems, to formulas, to comforting escapes. It is a fact that you are the world, and you are responsible for this aching confusion, and our talks must be based on this fact. Because you are the problem and there is no independent problem apart from you, you have to understand yourself if you would bring peace and order. When you are aware of this fact, you have to act positively and vigorously, and because you are afraid of such an action, you look to systems and to leaders. The only essential and starting point is you. Your individual responsibility is denied, smothered, by giving importance to systems, whether the left or the right or whether it be religious. Systems or formulas to save man become more important than man himself, than you. Organized society takes away individual responsibility; it makes him conform. And society, the state, becomes more important than the individual; through bureaucracy, the boredom of office and routine, the individual creative responsibility is slowly destroyed. The organized religion of dogma and belief saps away individual responsibility and freedom; through belief and dogma, the individual, you, feel secure, so you bring into being organized religion, the state, the system. Man, you, becomes unimportant through the efficiency of the machine, political or mechanical; the industry, the party, assume great significance, and you become merely a tool to be made efficient, to be a unit of a doctrine. This is happening to you, you are responsible for this death and irresponsibility, and yet you are not realizing this fact. Education, instead of awakening you to creative responsibility, is turning you out to be specialists along different lines: lawyers, police, army, and so on. You are educated and you cease to be an individual with deep significance. The more you are educated, the more you are conditioned; the more you read, the more you repeat, and so the less you are capable of revolutionary thinking. Regimentation, through the activities of society and state, education, army, and so on, is imposed upon you. So these and other factors make you a repetitive machine, unaware of your responsibility and significance.

To bring order and peace out of this darkness and misery, you have to start with yourself and not with the system, for psychologically, you are always the master of the machine, of the system. You are of the greatest significance and not the society nor the state, for you relationship with another is society; what you think, what you feel, what you do is of the utmost importance, for you create the environment, the state.

Collected Works, vol. IV, pp. 87-9
Madras, October 26, 1947

I think it is a great mistake to say that our problems are to be solved through collective or mass action

It must be fairly obvious to most of us that a different kind of thinking and action must be brought about in the world, and that requires very careful observation of ourselves, not mere analysis, but deep penetration into the activities of each one of us. The problems of our daily existence are numerous, and we have not the means or the capacity to deal with them; and as our lives are so drab, dull, and stupid, we try to escape from them, either intellectually or mystically. Intellectually we become cynical, clever, and very learned, or mystically we try to develop some powers or follow some guru, hoping to make our hearts more lovely and give our life more zest. Or, seeing the drabness of our life and the implication of our problems, and seeing that the problems are always on the increase, always multiplying, we think that to bring about a fundamental change, we cannot act as individuals, but must act in a mass, collectively. I think it is a great mistake to say that our problems are to be solved through collective or mass action. We believe that individual action is of very little importance and has no place when the problems are so vast, so complex, so demanding; therefore, we turn to collective or mass action. We think that if you and I acted individually, it would have very little result, so we join mass movements and take part in collective action. But if we examine collective action very closely, we will see that it is really based on you and me. We seem to regard mass action as the only effective action because it can produce a result, but we forget that individual action is much more effective, because the mass is composed of many individuals, the mass is not an independent entity, it is not different or separate from you and me.

So, what is important is to understand that any creative, any definitely effective action can be brought about only by individuals, that is, by you and me. Mass action is really an invention of the politician, is it not? It is a fictitious action in which there is no independent thought and action on the part of the individual. If you look at history, all great movements which resulted in collective action began with individuals like you and me, individuals who are capable of thinking very clearly and seeing things as they are; those individuals, through their understanding, invite others, and then there is collective action. After all, the collective is composed of individuals, and it is only the response of the individual, of you and me, that can bring about a fundamental alteration in the world; but when the individual does not see his responsibility, he throws the responsibility onto the collective, and the collective is then used by the clever politician, or by the clever religious leader. Whereas, if you see that you and I are responsible for the alteration of the conditions in the world, then the individual becomes extraordinarily important and not merely an instrument, a tool, in the hands of another.

So, you, the individual, are part of society you are not separate from society; what you are, society is. Though society may be an entity apart from you, you have created it, and therefore you alone can change it. But instead of realizing our responsibility as individuals in the collective, we as individuals become cynical, intellectual, or mystical; we avoid our responsibility towards definite action, which must be revolutionary in the fundamental sense; and as long as the individual, which is you and I, does not take responsibility for the complete transformation of society, society will remain as it is.

We seem to forget that the world problem is the individual problem, that the problems of the world are created by you and me as individuals. The problems of war, starvation, exploitation, and all the other in numerable problems that confront each one of us are created by you and me, and as long as we do not understand ourselves at every level, we will maintain the rottenness of the present society. So, before you can alter society, you have to understand what your whole structure is the manner of your thinking, the manner of your action, the ways of your relationship with people, ideas, and things. Revolution in society must begin with revolution in your own thinking and acting. The understanding of yourself is of primary importance if you would bring about a radical transformation in society, and the understanding of yourself is self-knowledge. Now, we have made self-knowledge into something extra ordinarily difficult and remote. Religions have made self-knowledge very mystical, abstract, and far away, but if you look at it more closely, you will see that self-knowledge is very simple and demands simple attention in relationship—and it is essential if there is to be a fundamental revolution in the structure of society. If you, the individual, do not understand the ways of your own thought and activities, merely to bring about a superficial revolution in the outer structure of society is to create further confusion and misery. If you do not know yourself, if you follow another without knowing the whole process of your own thinking and feeling, you will obviously be led to further confusion, to further disaster.

After all, life is relationship, and without relationship there is no possibility of life. There is no living in isolation, because living is a process of relationship, and relationship is not with abstractions; it is your relationship to property, to people, and to ideas. In relationship you see your self as you are, whatever you are, ugly or beautiful, subtle or gross; in the mirror of relationship you see precisely every new problem, the whole structure of yourself as you are. Because you think that you cannot alter your relationship fundamentally, you try to escape intellectually or mystically, and this escape only creates more problems, more confusion, and more disaster. But if, instead of escaping, you look at your life in relationship and under stand the whole structure of that relationship, then there is a possibility of going beyond that which is very close. Surely, to go very far, you must begin very near, but to begin near is very difficult for most of us because we want to escape from *what is,* from the fact of what we are. Without understanding ourselves, we cannot go far, and we are in constant relationship, there is no existence at all without relationship. So, relationship is the immediate, and to go beyond the immediate, there must be the understanding of relationship. But we would much rather examine that which is very far away, that which we call God or truth, than bring about a fundamental revolution in our relationship, and this escape to God or to truth is utterly fictitious, unreal. Relationship is the only thing that we have, and without under standing that relationship we can never find out what reality is or God is. So, to bring about a complete change in the social structure, in society, the individual must cleanse his relationship, and the cleansing of relationship is the beginning of his own transformation.

Collected Works, vol. VI, pp. 135-7
Bombay, March 14, 1950

I see that any revolution—economic, social, scientific—only affects the periphery, the outward boundaries of my mind; but inwardly I am still the same

As society exists now, man's relationship to man is organized; in that there is disorder because we are in conflict, not only within ourselves but with each other: as communities dividing themselves linguistically, nationally, religiously; dividing itself as family opposed to a community, the community opposed to a nation, and so on—outwardly. Inwardly, there is a tremendous urge to succeed, to compete, to conform; there is the drive of ambition, the despair, the boredom of everyday existence, and the despair of every human being when he discovers himself to be utterly, irredeemably lonely.

All this, consciously or unconsciously, is the battleground of relationship. Unless we bring order in that relationship, whatever the economic, the social, or the scientific revolution may produce, it will inevitably disintegrate, because the whole structure of the human mind has not been understood and resolved and made free.

So our problem is that we are responsible to bring about a complete psychological revolution because each one, each human being, is part of society, is not separate from society. There is no such thing as an individual. He may have a name, a separate family, and all the rest of it, but, psychologically, he is not an individual because he is conditioned by his society, by his beliefs, his fears, his dogmas, all those influences which are exercised by society, by the circumstances in which he lives. That is fairly obvious. He is conditioned by the society in which he lives, and the society in which he lives is created by him. He is responsible for that society, and he alone, as a human being, must bring about a transformation in that society.

And that is the greatest responsibility of every human being—not to join certain social reforms; that is totally inadequate, totally absurd; that is a fancy of some people according to their eccentric ideas. What we, as human beings, have to do—and to do this is our responsibility—is to bring about a psychological revolution, so that the relationship between man and man is based on order. That order can only come about through a psychological revolution, and this revolution can only come about when each one of us becomes gravely and tremendously responsible.

Most of us feel that someone else will bring about this revolution; that circumstances, God, beliefs, politicians, prayers, reading some books called the "sacred books," and so on will somehow transform our minds—that is, we shift our responsibility to someone else, to some leader, to some social pattern, to some influence. Such ways of thinking show an utter irresponsibility and also a great sense of indolence.

So this is your problem. I am not imposing this problem on you. You may not be aware of it, and the speaker is merely trying to point it out to you; he is not imposing the problem on you. If you are not hungry, no amount of anybody else's saying that you are hungry will make you hungry; but to be healthily hungry, your body must have a great deal of exercise. You have to be aware of this problem: that economic, political, scientific revolution is not the answer; that no leader, however tyrannical or beneficial, no authority, can bring about psychological order except you yourself, as a human being—not in the world of heaven, even if there is such a world, but in this world, and now.

So it is your problem. You may not want it. You may say, "I wish somebody else will show me the way; I will easily follow." Because we are used to following people—in the past, religious teachers; now it is Marx, or your particular guru, or some saint with his peculiar idiosyncrasies—we are always bound to authority. A mind enslaved by authority for centuries, through tradition, through custom, through habit—such a mind is willing to follow and therefore shifts the responsibility on to somebody else; such a mind cannot, under any circumstances, bring about psychological order. And that psychological order is imperative because we must lay the foundation in our daily life—that is the only thing that matters. From there, from the solid foundation, you can go very far. But if you have no foundation, or if you have laid your foundation on belief, on dogma, on authority, in the trust of some one else, then you are completely lost.

So we have to bring about a psychological transformation in our relationship with the society in which we live. Therefore, there is no escape from it into the Himalayas, into becoming a monk or a nun, and taking up social service and all the rest of such juvenile business. We have to live in this world; we have to bring about a radical transformation in our relationship with each other, not in some distant future, but now; and that is our greatest responsibility. Because if you cannot alter the psyche, the inward structure of your mind and heart, then you will be everlastingly in confusion, misery, and despair.

So, if it is a problem to you, not imposed by me, and if you are at all alert, if you are at all taking note of everything that is happening in the world, inevitably you will have this problem facing you. You may run away from it and, therefore, become irresponsible. But if it is a problem to you—as it must be to every thoughtful, intelligent, sensitive human being—then the problem is: How is one to bring about this radical transformation in the psyche, in the psychological structure of the human mind?

I, as a human being, am living in a particular society, and that society is not different from me. I am part of that society, I am conditioned by that society. That society has encouraged my greed, envy, jealousy, ambition, brutality; and I have contributed to that society my brutality, my ambition. We are both in it. I am part of it, I am part of the psychological structure of that society, which is me. Now, how am I to bring about a tremendous revolution within myself?

I see that any revolution—economic, social, scientific—only affects the periphery, the outward boundaries of my mind but inwardly I am still the same. I may put on different clothes, acquire different forms of technological knowledge, work only a few hours in a week, and so on. But inwardly, I am still in conflict; I am still ambitious, frustrated, under a terrific strain. Unless there is a tremendous transformation there, I cannot be orderly in living; there can be no freedom, no happiness, no escape from sorrow.

Collected Works, vol. XV, pp. 56-8
Bombay, February 14, 1965

The social pattern is set up by man; it is not independent of man, though it has a life of its own, and man is not independent of it; they are interrelated. Change within the pattern is no change at all; it is mere modification, reformation. Only by breaking away from the social pattern without building another can you 'help' society. As long as you belong to society, you are only helping it to deteriorate. All societies including the most marvellously utopian, have within them the seeds of their own corruption. To change society, you must break away from it. You must cease to be what society is: acquisitive, ambitious, envious, power-seeking, and so on.

Commentaries On Living, Series III, p. 82

The psychological structure of society is far more important than the organizational side of society

And as we were saying, man is responsible—you are responsible, and I—for the condition of the society in which we live. You are responsible, not your politicians, because you have made the politicians what they are—crooked, glorifying themselves, seeking position and prestige—which is what we are doing in daily life. We are responsible for society. The psychological structure of society is far more important than the organizational side of society. The psychological structure of society is based on greed, envy, acquisitiveness, competition, ambition, fear, this incessant demand of a human being wanting to be secure in all his relationships, secure in property, secure in his relationship to people, secure in his relationship to ideas. That is the structure of society which one has created. And society then imposes the structure psychologically on each one of us. Now greed, envy, ambition, competition—all that is a waste of energy because in it there is always a conflict, conflict which is endless as in a person who is jealous.

As we are responsible for the misery, for the poverty, for wars, for the utter lack of peace, a religious man does not seek God. The religious man is concerned with the transformation of society which is himself. The religious man is not the man that does innumerable rituals, follows traditions, lives in a dead, past culture, explaining endlessly the Gita or the Bible, endlessly chanting, or taking *sanyasa* —that is not a religious man; such a man is escaping from facts. The religious man is concerned totally and completely with the understanding of society which is himself. He is not separate from society. Bringing about in himself a complete, total mutation means complete cessation of greed, envy, ambition; and therefore he is not dependent on circumstances, though he is the result of circumstances—the food he eats, the books he reads, the cinemas he goes to, the religious dogmas, beliefs, rituals, and all that business. He is responsible, and therefore the religious man must understand himself, who is the product of society which he himself has created. Therefore to find reality he must begin here, not in a temple, not in an image—whether the image is graven by the hand or by the mind. Otherwise how can he find something totally new, a new state?

Collected Works, vol. XV, pp. 90-1
Bombay, March 3, 1965

IV.   On Politics

**We want to bring order within society, but how are we to do
it?**

*Question: ...since the major causes of catastrophe in the world
arise from malfunctioning social organization, is there not danger
in over-emphasizing the need for the individuals to change themselves, even though the change is ultimately necessary?*

Krishnamurti: What is society? Is it not the relationship of one
individual with another? If individuals in themselves are ignorant,
cruel, ambitious, and so on, their society will reflect all that they are
in themselves. The questioner seems to suggest that the conflicting
relationship of individuals, which is society, with its many organizations, should be changed. We all see the necessity, the importance
of social change. Wars, starvation, ruthless pursuit of power, and
so on—with these we are all familiar, and some earnestly desire to
change these conditions. How are you going to change them? By
destroying the many or the few who create the disharmony in the
world? Who are the many or the few? You and I, aren't we? Each
one is involved in it because we are greedy, we are possessive, we
crave for power. We want to bring order within society, but how
are we to do it? Do you seriously think there are only a few who
are responsible for this social disorganization, these wars and
hatreds? How are you going to get rid of them? If you destroy
them, you use the very means they have employed and so make of
yourself also an instrument of hatred and brutality. Hate cannot be
destroyed by hate, however much you may like to hide your hate

under pleasant sounding words. Methods determine the ends. You cannot kill in order to have peace and order; to have peace you must create peace within yourself and thereby in your relationship with others, which is society.

You say that more emphasis should be laid on changing the social organization. Superficial reforms can, perhaps, be made, but surely radical change or lasting peace can be brought about only when the individual himself changes. You may say that this will take a long time. Why are you concerned about time? In your eagerness you want immediate results, you are concerned with results and not with the ways and means; thus in your haste you become a plaything of empty promises. Do you think that the present human nature which has been the product of centuries of maltreatment, ignorance, fear can be altered overnight? A few individuals may be able to change themselves overnight, but not a crystallized society. This does not mean a postponing, but the man who thinks clearly, directly, is not concerned with time.

Social organization may be an independent mechanism, but it has to be run by us. We have created it and we are responsible for it, and we can be independent of it only when we, as individuals, do not contribute to the general hate, greed, ambition, and so on. In our desire to change the world we always meet with opposition—groups are formed for and against, which only further engender antagonism, suspicion, and competition in conversion. Agreement is almost impossible except when there is common hate or fear; all actions born of fear and hate must further increase fear and hate. Lasting order and peace can be brought about only when the individual voluntarily and intelligently consents to think without hate, greed, ambition, and so on. Only in this way can there be creative peace within you and therefore in your relationship with another, which is called society.

Collected Works, vol. III, pp. 152-3
Ojai, California, June 2, 1940

Our problem is not feeding, clothing, and shelter alone

Question: How can individual regeneration alone possibly bring about, in the immediate, the collective well-being of the greatest number, which is the need everywhere?

Krishnamurti: We think that individual regeneration is opposed to collective regeneration. We are not thinking in terms of regeneration, but only of individual regeneration. Regeneration is anonymous. It is not, "I have redeemed myself." As long as you think of individual regeneration as being opposed to the collective, then there is no relationship between the two. But if you are concerned with regeneration, not of the individual, but *regeneration,* then you will see there is quite a different force—intelligence—at work; because after all, what are we concerned with? What is the question with which we are concerned, profoundly and deeply? One might see the necessity for united action of man to save man. He sees that collective action is necessary in order to produce food, clothing, and shelter. That requires intelligence, and intelligence is not individual, is not of this party or that party, this country or that country. If the individual seeks intelligence, it will be collective. But unfortunately, we are not seeking intelligence, we are not seeking the solution of this problem. We have theories of our problems, ways of how to solve them, and the ways become individual and collective. If you and I seek an intelligent way to the problem, then we are not collective or individual; then we are concerned with intelligence that will solve the problem.

What is collective, what is mass? You in relationship with another, is it not? This is not oversimplification because in my relationship with you, I form a society; you and I together create a society in our relationship. Without that relationship, there is no intelligence, there is no cooperation on your side or on my side that is wholly individual. If I seek my regeneration and you seek your regeneration, what happens? We, both of us, are pursuing opposite directions.

If both of us are concerned with the intelligent solution of the whole problem because that problem is our main concern, then our concern is not how I look at it or you look at it, not my path or your path; we are not concerned with frontiers or economic bias, with vested interests and stupidity which come into being with those vested interests. Then you and I are not collective, are not individual; this brings about collective integration which is anonymous.

But the questioner wants to know how to act immediately, what to do the next moment, so that man's needs can be solved. I am afraid there is no such answer. There is no immediate moral remedy, whatever politicians may promise. The immediate solution is the regeneration of the individual, not for himself, but regeneration which is the awakening of intelligence. Intelligence is not yours or mine; it is intelligence. I think it is important to see this deeply. Then our political and individual action, collective or otherwise, will be quite different. We shall lose our identity; we shall not identify ourselves with something—our country, our race, our group, our collective traditions, our prejudices. We shall lose all those things because the problem demands that we shall lose our identity in order to solve it. But that requires great, comprehensive understanding of the whole problem.

Our problem is not the bread and butter problem alone. Our problem is not feeding, clothing, and shelter alone, but it is more profound than that. It is a psychological problem, why man identifies himself. And it is this identification with a party, with a religion, with knowledge, that is dividing us. And that identity can be resolved only when, psychologically, the whole process of identifying, the desire, the motive, is clearly understood.

So the problem of the collective or of the individual is non-existent when you are pursuing the solution of a particular problem. If you and I are both interested in something, vitally interested in the solution of the problem, we shall not identify ourselves with something else. But unfortunately, as we are not vitally interested, we have identified ourselves, and it is that identity that is preventing us from resolving this complex and vast problem.

Collected Works, vol. VI, pp. 296-7
Madras, January 27, 1952

There must be radical change in the political field; but such a change will have no depth if I do not pursue the other

Question: Can I, who am religiously inclined and desirous of acting wholly and integrally, express myself through politics? For, to me, it appears that a radical change is necessary in the political field?

Krishnamurti: What the questioner means is this: seeking wholly, seeking religiously the whole, entire, complete, can I politically function, that is, act partially? He says politics is obviously the path for him; when he seeks and follows that path which is not the whole, complete, he merely functions in fields which are partial, fragmentary. Is that not so? What is your answer, not your cunning answer or immediate response? Can I see the whole thing of life, which means, can I love? Let us take love. I have compassion; I feel tremendously and for the whole; can I then act only politically? Can I, seeking the whole, be a Hindu or a Brahmin? Can I, having love in my heart, identify myself with a path, with a particular country, with a particular system—economic or religious? Suppose I want to improve the particular, I want to bring about a radical change in the particular, in the country in which I live; the moment I identify myself with that particular, have

I not shut out the whole? This is your problem just as mine. We are thinking about it together. You are not listening to me. When we are trying to find an answer, your opinions and ideas are not the solution. What we are trying to find is, can a truly religious man—not a phoney one that consults others—a really sacred person seeking the whole, can he identify himself with a radical movement for a particular country? And will it do to have revolution—don't be afraid of that word—of one country, of one people, of one state, if I am seeking the whole, if I am trying to understand that which is not within the scope of the mind? Can I, using my mind, act politically? I see there must be political action; I see there must be real change, radical change in our relationship, in our economic system, in the distribution of land, and so on. I see there must be revolution, and yet at the same time, I am pursuing a path, the political path; I am also trying to understand the whole. What is my action there? Is not that your problem, sirs? Can you act politically —that is, partially—and understand the whole? Politics and economics are partial; they are not the whole, integrated life; they are partial, necessary, essential. Can I abandon the whole or leave the whole society and tinker with the particular? Obviously, I cannot. But I can act upon it, not through it.

We want to bring about a certain change; we have certain ideas about it; we pursue so many groups and so on. We use means to achieve the result. And is the understanding of the whole contrary to that? Am I confusing you? I am only telling you what I think; do not accept it, but think it out for yourself and see. For me, political action, economic action are of secondary importance though they are essential. There must be radical change in the political field, but such a change will have no depth if I do not pursue the other. If the other is not primary, if the other is only secondary, then my action towards the secondary will have tremendous significance. But, if I see a certain path and act politically, political action becomes important to me, and not acting integrally. But, if acting integrally is really important to me and if I pursue it, political action, religious action, economic action, will come rightly, deeply, fundamentally. If I do not pursue the other but merely confine myself to the political, the economic, or the social change, then I create more misery.

So it all depends on what you lay emphasis on. Laying emphasis on the right thing—which is the whole—will produce its own action with regard to politics and so on. It all depends on you. In pursuing that whole thing without saying, "I am going to act politically or socially," you will bring about fundamental alterations politically, religiously, and economically.

Collected Works, vol. VI, pp. 277-8
Madras, January 19, 1952

Why do specialists take charge of our lives?

Question: One sees that chaos in the world is rapidly increasing. Billions are being spent on arms, social justice is being eroded, governments, both totalitarian and democratic are increasingly aggressive, and violent. Though one sees the necessity of much deeper fundamental human change, could the speaker comment on the issue of active political involvement?

Krishnamurti: Am I Democratic or Republican, is that it? Apart from joking, why, if one may ask, why do we have such great confidence in political leaders? This is the same issue in all countries, in France, in England, here, in India, and so on. Why? We put such confidence in the economists, in the politicians, in the leaders. Why do we do this? And what do we mean by political action?

Please, we are enquiring together, you are not just listening to the speaker, waiting for his explanation and answer. We are thinking together over this problem which is really a very serious problem, which is affecting the whole of mankind. Some political group comes into power, Democratic, Conservative or Labour, or Republican or Democrat; they seem to have such extraordinary power, position and authority, and we follow them. They tell us what to do and we accept them. Why is there that sense of trust in them and acceptance their judgments? We are sent to war by rulers, government officials, and thousands are being killed. Because a majority have voted them into power, they set position and direction and we merely follow them like sheep. Generally they appeal to our lowest instincts, to our national pride, honour, and all that business. And we are stimulated by all that and we are willing to kill others for this, for a piece of land, and so on. Why? Why do we trust them?

Please, you answer this question. And what do we mean by political action which is different from all other actions? Why do we separate politics from our daily living? Why do we separate political activity of the left, right, centre, or extreme left, extreme right? Why, if one may ask, is political action so very different from our action of relationship, action with regard to fear in ourselves, and so on? Or is politics part of our life, not something separate. Then politics, according to the common usage which is in the dictionary, is the art of government, science of government. Why do we give this art to the politician?

They apparently are a separate breed, different from us. This is really a question that involves us: Why do we depend on a politician, a guru, a priest, on anybody to govern us? Please answer this question. Why do specialists take charge of our lives? Is it that we have no so-called confidence in ourselves? We are not sure of ourselves? And we attribute this clarity to the politicians and to the others. Is it that in ourselves we are insufficient and somebody out there is going to make us sufficient?

Are we to treat life as separate factors, political, religious, economic, and so on? Or are we to treat life as a whole? Please, question this. The questioner asks what political action one can take? Is that political action different from religious action, from the action of an idealist? Or does one treat life as the whole of living: learning, relationship, fears, faith, anxiety, and political action? Isn't that a whole way of living?

Is it that we are so fragmented in ourselves as religious action, political action, family action, individual action, collective action? Or do we treat life as a total movement in which all these activities are included. But if we separate one from the other, we inevitably bring about contradiction. A religious life is incompatible, one would say, with political life; a religious person will have no part with politics, because generally politics is such a crooked affair, controlled by big industrialists, by wanting a great deal of money for the party, and depending on rich people, and so on. So how do we, each one of us, answer this question? There is increase of armaments; just now they are destroying each other, killing each other for god knows what. And both the democratic world and the totalitarian world are becoming, as the questioner says, more and more aggressive.

So how do you deal with this question? It's very easy to put questions and try to find an answer from another. But if we have to answer this question ourselves, taking what is actually going on in the world—the national, religious, economic divisions, wars, tremendous spending of money on armaments—what is your answer? If you are American, you say, our way is the best way. Would you consider the right answer, the true answer is that we cannot separate these activities but treat life as a whole movement?

And what is a political action? Would you like to start a new party, a social democratic party, or look for a new leader for the next election? Condemn the present leader, and when a new leader comes into being in the next election, again there is doubt about him. You know, the whole thing: when the honeymoon is over, then begins the whole problem. What is your answer? Please, sirs, go into it for yourselves; what is your answer when you have thought it out deeply? Do you want to ask if there is an activity, if there is action, which is not divisible, an action that includes politics, religion, economics, everything, the whole bundle of life. And is that possible?

One sees corruption right through the world: black markets, rich people getting tremendously more rich, the privileged classes, and so on. Where do you begin to bring about an action that will include all actions? Where do you begin? To go very far, one must begin very near. Right? So what is very near? Me. I am the nearest person, so I begin—not as a selfish activity, or self-centred movement. I am the nearest, or I am the centre from which I start, not out there. Can I live a life that is absolutely not broken up? Not a religious life separate from all other lives, activities, but a life that is political, religious—do you follow? Can I live that way?

That implies, doesn't it, that I understand the whole separative activity completely and comprehend that the separate activities then become contradictory, conflicting, endless divisions. If I understand that very clearly, perceive it not as an abstraction or as an ideal but as an actual fact, then from that observation there will be an action which will be complete. If you are actually wanting to start a political action, a new party, a new group, a new leader of your own, then I am afraid you and I won't meet; we are back into the same old pattern. We are saying that from that quality of a mind and heart of a life that is complete, sufficient psychologically, all action is included.

Saanen, Switzerland, July 29, 1981

What we are concerned with is not reformation or modified continuity, but the fundamental transformation of man in his relationship with man

Question: Why don't you participate in politics or in social reform?

Krishnamurti: Have you noticed how politics and social reform have become extraordinarily predominant in our lives at the present time? All our newspapers and most of the magazines, except the purely escapist ones, are full of politics, economics, and other problems. Have you ever asked yourself why they are that way, why human beings are giving such extraordinary importance to politics, economics, and social reform? Reforms are obviously necessary because of the economic, social, and political confusion and the general deterioration of the state of man following the two wars. So, crowds gather round political leaders; people line the streets, watching them as though they were strange animals trying to solve the problem on the economic, social, or political level, independent of the total process of man. Are these problems to be tackled separately, unrelated to the whole psychological problem of man? You may have a perfect system that you think will solve the economic problems of the world, but another will also have a perfect system, and the two systems, representing two different ideologies, will fight each other. As long as you are fighting over ideas, systems, there cannot be a true, radical revolution, there cannot be fundamental social transformation. Ideas do not transform people. What brings about transformation is freedom from ideas. Revolution based on ideas is no longer revolution but merely a continuation of the past in a modified state. Obviously, that is not revolution.

The questioner wants to know why I don't take part in politics or in social reform. Surely, if you can understand the total process of man, then you are dealing with the fundamental issues, not merely trimming particular branches of the tree. But most of us are not interested in the entire problem. We are concerned merely with reconciliation, superficial adjustment, not with the fundamental understanding of man as a total process. It is very much easier to be an expert on one particular level. The experts on the economic or political level leave the psychological level to other experts, and so we become slaves to experts; we are sacrificed by experts for an idea. So, there can be fundamental revolution only in understanding the total process of yourself, not as an individual opposed to the mass, to society, but as an individual interrelated with society; because without you there is no society, without you there is no relationship with another. There is no revolution, no fundamental transformation, as long as we do not understand ourselves. Reformers and so-called revolutionists are really factors of retrogression in society. A reformer tries to patch up the present society, or create a new one, on the basis of an ideology, and his idea is the conditioned response to a pattern; and such revolution, based on an ideology, can never produce a fundamental, radical transformation in social relationships. What we are concerned with is not reformation or modified continuity, which you call revolution, but the fundamental transformation of man in his relationship with man; and as long as that basic change does not take place in the individual, we cannot produce a new social order. That fundamental transformation does not depend on belief, on religious organizations, or on any political or economic system—it depends on your understanding of yourself in relationship with another. That is the real revolution that must take place, and then you as an individual will have an extraordinary influence in society. But without that transformation, merely to talk about revolution or to sacrifice yourself for a so-called practical idea—which is not really sacrifice at all—is obviously mere repetition, which is retrogression.

Collected Works, vol. VI, pp. 66-7
Colombo, Sri Lanka, January 15, 1950

To act collectively we must begin individually

Question: Why don't you face the economic and social evils instead of escaping into some dark, mystical affair?

Krishnamurti: I have been trying to point out that only by giving importance to those things that are primary can the secondary issues be understood and solved. Economic and social evils are not to be adjusted without understanding what causes them. To understand them and so bring about a fundamental change, we have first to comprehend ourselves who are the cause of these evils. We have, individually and so as a group, created social and economic strife and confusion. We alone are responsible for them and thus we, individually and so perhaps collectively, can bring order and clarity. To act collectively we must begin individually; to act as a group each one must understand and change radically those causes within himself which produce the outer conflict and misery. Through legislation you may gain certain beneficial results, but without altering the inner, fundamental causes of conflict and antagonism they will be overturned and confusion will rise again; outer reforms will ever need further reform and this way leads to oppression and violence. Lasting outer order and creative peace can come about only if each one brings order and peace within himself.

Collected Works, vol. III, p. 226
Ojai, California, June 25, 1944

Why isn't there a group of people sitting together trying to solve the problems of nationalism?

Question: Why do you waste your time preaching instead of helping the world in a practical way?

Krishnamurti: Now, what do you mean by "practical"? You mean bringing about a change in the world, a better economic adjustment, a better distribution of wealth, a better relationship—or, to put it more brutally, helping you to find a better job. You want to see a change in the world—every intelligent man does—and you want a method to bring about that change, and therefore you ask me why I waste my time preaching instead of doing something about it. Now, is what I am actually doing a waste of time? It would be a waste of time, would it not, if I introduced a new set of ideas to replace the old ideology, the old pattern. Perhaps that is what you want me to do. But instead of pointing out a so-called practical way to act, to live, to get a better job, to create a better world, is it not important to find out what are the impediments which actually prevent a real revolution—not a revolution of the left or the right, but a fundamental, radical revolution, not based on ideas? Because, as we have discussed it, ideals, beliefs, ideologies, dogmas, prevent action. There cannot be a world transformation, a revolution, as long as action is based on ideas because action then is merely reaction; therefore, ideas become much more important than action, and that is precisely what is taking place in the world, isn't it? To act, we must discover the impediments that prevent action. But most of us don't want to act—that is our difficulty. We prefer to discuss, we prefer to substitute one ideology for another, and so we escape from action through ideology. Surely, that is very simple, is it not? The world at the present time is facing many problems: overpopulation, starvation, division of people into nationalities and classes, and so on. Why isn't there a group of people sitting together trying to solve the problems of nationalism? But if we try to become international while clinging to our nationality, we create another problem, and that is what most of us do. So, you see that ideals are really preventing action. A statesman, an eminent authority, has said the world can be organized and all the people fed. Then why is it not done? Because of conflicting ideas, beliefs, and nationalisms. Therefore, ideas are actually preventing the feeding of people, and most of us play with ideas and think we are tremendous revolutionaries, hypnotizing ourselves with such words as *practical*. What is important is to free ourselves from ideas, from nationalisms, from all religious beliefs and dogmas, so that we can act, not according to a pattern or an ideology, but as needs demand; and, surely, to point out the hindrances and impediments that prevent such action is not a waste of time, is not a lot of hot air. What you are doing is obviously nonsense. Your ideas and beliefs, your political, economic, and religious panaceas, are actually dividing people and leading to war. It is only when the mind is free of idea and belief that it can act rightly. A man who is patriotic, nationalistic, can never know what it is to be brotherly, though he may talk about it; on the contrary, his actions, economically and in every direction, are conducive to war. So, there can be right action and therefore radical, lasting transformation, only when the mind is free of ideas, not superficially, but fundamentally, and freedom from ideas can take place only through self-awareness and self-knowledge.

Collected Works, vol. VI, pp. 54-5
Colombo, Sri Lanka, January 1, 1950

He who is eager to reform the world must first understand himself for he is the world

If the reformer, the contributor to the solution of the world's problems, has not radically transformed himself, if he has had no inner revolution of values, then what he contributes will only add further to conflict and misery. He who is eager to reform the world must first understand himself for he is the world. The present misery and degradation of man is brought on by man himself, and if he merely plans to reform the pattern of conflict without fundamentally understanding himself, he will only increase ignorance and sorrow.

Collected Works, vol. IV, p. 33
Ojai, California, July 8, 1945

There must also be workers of the other type

You think that work and assistance can help those who are suffering. To me such an attempt to do social good for the welfare of man is patchwork. I am not saying that it is wrong; it is undoubtedly necessary, because society is in a state which demands that there be those who work to bring about social change, those who work to better social conditions. But there must also be workers of the other type, those who work to prevent the new structures of society from being based on false ideas.

Collected Works, vol. I, p. 132
Oslo, Norway, September 10, 1933

To be alone is obviously to be in a state of revolution against the whole setup of society

So, the problem, Sir, is this: A mind that is not innocent can never receive that which is innocent. God, truth, or whatever the thing that is not nameable—the immeasurable—that cannot be without an innocent mind, without a mind that is dead to all the things of society, dead to power, position, prestige, dead to knowledge. After all, power, position, prestige is what we call living. For us, that is life; for us, that is action. You have to die to that action, and you cannot do it because that is what you want. Sir, to die to the things which we call living is the very living. If you go down that street and see the power, those flags which are the measures of power, and if you die to all that, it means that you die to your own demand for power which has created all this horror.

Comment: It is some sort of total annihilation.

Krishnamurti: Why not? What is living but total annihilation? Is the way you live now really living? Sir, we want to gain heaven without going through anything; we want to be mediocre human beings, completely comfortable and secure, and have our drinks and our sex and our power, and also have that thing which we call heaven.

So, sirs, to sum up: To be alone, which is not a philosophy of loneliness, is obviously to be in a state of revolution against the whole set-up of society—not only this society, but the communist society, the fascist, every form of society as organized brutality, organized power. And that means an extraordinary perception of the effects of power. Sir, have you noticed those soldiers rehearsing? They are not human beings any more, they are machines, they are your sons and my sons, standing there in the sun. This is happening here, in America, in Russia, and everywhere—not only at the governmental level, but also at the monastic level, belonging to monasteries, to orders, to groups who employ this astonishing power. And it is only such a mind that can be alone. And aloneness is not something to be cultivated. You see this? When you see all this, you are out, and no governor or president is going to invite you to dinner. Out of that aloneness there is humility. It is this aloneness that knows love—not power. The ambitious man, religious or ordinary, will never know what love is. So, if one sees all this, then one has this quality of total living and therefore total action. This comes through self-knowledge.

Collected Works, vol. XII, p. 40
New Delhi, January 20, 1961

V.   On War

War is the spectacular and bloody projection of our everyday life

Question: How can we solve our present political chaos and the crisis in the world? Is there anything an individual can do to stop the impending war?

Krishnamurti: War is the spectacular and bloody projection of our everyday life, is it not? War is merely an outward expression of our inward state, an enlargement of our daily action. It is more spectacular, more bloody, more destructive, but it is the collective result of our individual activities. Therefore, you and I are responsible for war and what can we do to stop it? Obviously the ever-impending war cannot be stopped by you and me, because it is already in movement; it is already taking place, though at present chiefly on the psychological level. As it is already in movement, it cannot be stopped—the issues are too many, too great, and are already committed. But you and I, seeing that the house is on fire, can understand the causes of that fire, can go away from it and build in a new place with different materials that are not combustible, that will not produce other wars. That is all that we can do. You and I can see what creates wars, and if we are interested in stopping wars, then we can begin to transform ourselves, who are the causes of war.

An American lady came to see me a couple of years ago, during the war. She said she had lost her son in Italy and that she had another son aged sixteen whom she wanted to save; so we talked the thing over. I suggested to her that to save her son she had to cease to be an American; she had to cease to be greedy, cease piling up wealth, seeking power, domination, and be morally simple—not merely simple in clothes, in outward things, but simple in her thoughts and feelings, in her relationships. She said, "That is too much. You are asking far too much. I cannot do it, because circumstances are too powerful for me to alter". Therefore she was responsible for the destruction of her son.

The First and Last Freedom, 182-3

Do you know how war has come into being? It has come because in our daily lives we destroy one another

Question: All except a few do not want war, so why do they prepare for war?

Krishnamurti: I am not at all sure that the majority do not want war. Do you know what war means? War means destruction— killing and maiming one another, with the noise, the brutality, the ugliness, the appalling misery of pain. You have seen it on the films; that is war. Do you know how war has come into being? It has come because in our daily lives we destroy one another. Though in the temple we talk about the love of God, in our business dealings we are cutting one another's throats. Also, we have wars because we have armies, and it is the purpose of an army to prepare for war. Do you mean to say that an army man would want to give up his position, his job, his money, in order to have peace? He would not be so stupid.

So all of us, in one way or the other, are preparing for war. You can prevent war only if, in your daily life, you realize that you are no longer a Hindu, a Christian, a Buddhist, a Muslim or a communist. If in your daily life you are kind, generous, affectionate, loving, then you will have a different world. Then, instead of squandering money on armaments, you can make this world into a paradise. But it is up to you. You have the government you deserve because you are part of that government, because you are politicians in your daily lives, and you want position, power, and authority.

Collected Works, vol. XVII, p. 280
Banaras, India, December 17, 1967

As you are responsible for war, you must be responsible for peace

As long as we use technological knowledge for the advancement and glorification of the individual or of the group, the needs of man can never be sanely and effectively organized. It is this desire for psychological security through technological advancement that is destroying the physical security of man. There is sufficient scientific knowledge to feed, clothe, and shelter man but the proper use of this knowledge is denied as long as there are separative nationalities with their sovereign governments and frontiers—which in turn give rise to class and racial strife. So, you are responsible for the continuance of this conflict between man and man. As long as you, the individual, are nationalistic and patriotic, as long as you hold to political and social ideologies, you are responsible for war because your relationship with another can only breed confusion and antagonism. Seeing the false as the false is the beginning of wisdom, and it is this truth alone that can bring happiness to you and so to the world.

As you are responsible for war, you must be responsible for peace. Those who creatively feel this responsibility must first free themselves psychologically from the causes of war and not merely plunge into organizing political peace groups—which will only breed further division and opposition.

Peace is not an idea opposed to war. Peace is a way of life, for there can be peace only when everyday living is understood. It is only this way of life that can effectively meet the challenge of war, of class, and of ever-increasing technological advancement. This way of life is not the way of the intellect. The worship of the intellect in opposition to life has led us all to our present frustration with its innumerable escapes. These escapes have become far more important than the understanding of the problem itself. The present crisis has come into being because of the worship of the intellect, and it is the intellect that has divided life into a series of opposing and contradictory actions; it is the intellect that has denied the unifying factor which is love. The intellect has filled the empty heart with the things of the mind, and it is only when the mind is aware of its own reasoning and is able to go beyond itself, that there can be the enrichment of the heart.

Collected Works, vol. V, p. 153
New Delhi, November 6, 1948

To have peace, you must live peacefully; that is, no ambition, no competition, no nationality, no class division, no petty little division of race, of country—linguistic or nonlinguistic. To live peacefully you must be at peace with yourself. And if you cannot be at peace with yourself, it is no good praying for peace, because everything that you are doing is bringing about disorder, bringing about conflict.

Collected Works, vol. XV, p. 84
Bombay, February 28, 1965

Surely, a people survive only when they can meet the challenge anew; otherwise they are destroyed

Now, is this vast problem of the world your problem and my problem, or is it independent of us? Is war independent of you? Is the national strife independent of you, the communal strife independent of you? The corruption, the degradation, the moral disintegration—are they independent of each one of us? This disintegration is directly related to us, and therefore the responsibility rests with each one of us. Surely, that is the main problem, isn't it? That is, to put it differently: Is the problem to be left to the few leaders, either of the left or the right, to the party, to the discipline, to an ideology, to the United Nations, to the expert, to the specialist? Or is it a problem that directly involves us, which means: Are we directly responsible for these problems, or are we not? Surely, that is the issue, is it not? Perhaps, many of you may not have thought about this; therefore, it may be quite strange to you, but the question is, is it not, whether the individual problem is the world problem, whether you can do anything about it?—the religious collapse, the moral collapse, the political corruption, the so-called independence that has produced nothing but decay. Is it your problem, or do you leave it all to chance or wait for some miracle to happen so that it will produce a revolution? Or do you leave it to some authority, to a political party, of the left or of the right? What is your response? Don't you have to solve it, don't you have to attack it, don't you have to respond vitally to a challenge of this kind? I am not being rhetorical but merely factual; this is no place for rhetoric, that would be absurd. There is a challenge given to us all the time; life is a challenge. And do we respond, and according to what conditioning do we respond? And when we do respond, is that response capable of meeting the challenge?

So, to meet this world catastrophe, this world crisis, this enormous unprecedented challenge, have we not to discover how we, individually, respond? Because, after all, a society is the relationship between you and me and an other. There is no society which is not founded on relationship. What you and I and another are, is the society, surely. And have we not to understand that relationship between you and me and another in order to transform society, in order to bring about a revolution—a complete, radical transformation? Because, obviously, that is what is needed—a revolution, not of the bloody kind, not of mere ideas, not based on ideas, but a revolution of fundamental value, not according to any pattern or ideology, but a revolution born out of the understanding of the relationship between you and me and another, which is society. So in order to bring about a fundamental, radical transformation in society, is it not our responsibility, our individual responsibility, to discover what is our direct response to this challenge? Do we respond as a Hindu or a Muslim or a Christian or a communist or a socialist? And is such response a valid response, a response which will bring about a fundamental change? I hope I am making the problem clear. If you respond to this world crisis, which is a new challenge, as a Hindu, surely you are not understanding the challenge. You are merely responding to the challenge, which is always new, according to an old pattern, and therefore, your response has no corresponding validity, newness, freshness. If you respond as a Catholic or a communist, again you are responding, are you not, according to a patterned thought. Therefore your response has no significance. And has not the Hindu, the Muslim, the Buddhist, the Christian, created this problem? As the new religion is the worship of the state, the old religion was the worship of an idea. So if you respond to a challenge according to an old conditioning, your response will not enable you to understand the new challenge. Therefore, what one has to do in order to meet the challenge is to strip oneself completely, denude oneself entirely of the background and meet the challenge anew. Surely, a state, a country, a civilization, and a people endure, last, survive only when they can meet the challenge anew; otherwise, they succumb, they are destroyed. And that is exactly what is happening. Technologically we are tremendously advanced, but morally, spiritually, we are very far behind. And with this lack of moral stamina, we meet this extraordinary technological progress, and therefore there is always a friction, a contradiction.

So, surely, our problem is, is it not, that there is this new challenge. And all leaders have failed—spiritual, moral, political— and leaders will always fail because we choose leaders out of our confusion, and any leader whom we choose will inevitably lead us to confusion. Sir, see the importance of it; don't brush it aside as a clever statement. See the danger of a leader, not only politically, but religiously. Because, the one whom we choose for a leader is chosen out of our confusion. Because I am confused, I do not know what to do, how to act, I come to you, and because I am confused I choose you. If I am clear, I will not choose you; I do not want a leader because I am a light unto myself—I can think out my problems for myself. It is only when I am confused that I go to another. I may call him a guru, a mahatma, a political leader, and so on, but I go to him because of my confusion. I only see through the darkness of my own confusion.

A man who earnestly wishes to investigate the whole catastrophic problem of sorrow must begin with himself. It is only through creative understanding of ourselves that there can be a creative world, a happy world, a world in which ideas do not exist.

Collected Works, vol. V, pp. 182-3
Banaras, India, January 16, 1949

What is civilization? It is an expression of the collective will, is it not?

Question: Are individuals impotent against the atomic and hydrogen bombs?

Krishnamurti: They are going on experimenting with these bombs in America, in Russia, and elsewhere, and what can you and I do about it? So what is the point of discussing this matter? You may try to create public opinion by writing to the papers about how terrible it is, but will that stop the governments from investigating and creating the H-bomb? Are they not going to go on with it anyhow? They may use atomic energy for peaceful as well as destructive purposes, and probably within five or ten years they will have factories running on atomic energy, but they will also be preparing for war. They may limit the use of atomic weapons, but the momentum of war is there, and what can we do? Historical events are in movement, and I don't think you and I living here in Benaras can stop that movement. Who is going to care? But what we can do is something completely different. We can step out of the present machinery of society which is constantly preparing for war, and perhaps by our own total inward revolution, we shall be able to contribute to the building of a civilization which is altogether new.

After all, what is civilization? What is the Indian or the European civilization? It is an expression of the collective will, is it not? The will of the many has created this present civilization in India, and cannot you and I break away from it and think entirely differently about these matters? Is it not the responsibility of serious people to do this? Must there not be serious people who see this process of destruction going on in the world, who investigate it, and who step out of it in the sense of not being ambitious and all the rest of it? What else can we do? But you see, we are not willing to be serious, that is the difficulty. We don't want to tackle ourselves, we want to discuss something outside, far away.

Collected Works, vol. VIII, p. 262
Banaras, India, January 9, 1955

This problem can only be resolved when you find out why you are angry, why you are violent

Question: Will there be an end to these evil wars and violence?

Krishnamurti: A little boy asks because he is concerned with the future, with tomorrow, with a world that is becoming more and more violent, with wars, and more wars. He says, "My future is being created by the older generation and they have produced these monstrous wars," and he asks, "Will there be an end to it?"

There will be an end only when you are nonviolent. You must begin as an individual—you cannot make the whole world non violent in a flash. Forget the world; be, as an individual, nonviolent. I do not know whether you have ever wondered what the older generation have done to this world. The older generation have produced this world of violence, greed, hatred; they are entirely responsible for it, not God. They have lived a life of brutality, self-concern, callousness. They have made this world, and the younger people say, "You have made a filthy world, an ugly world," and they are in revolt. And I am afraid their revolt will produce another form of violence, which is actually what is going on.

So, this problem can only be resolved—this problem of violence, of wars in the future—when you, as an individual, find out why you are angry, why you are violent, why you have prejudice, why you hate, and put them all away. You cannot put them away by revolting against them but only by understanding them. Understanding them means to look, to observe, to listen. When the older people talk about all the ugly things they have made, listen closely, give your attention, which means give your heart and your mind to this. You know, in the past five thousand years there have been about fifteen thousand wars, which means three wars every year. Though man has talked about love—love of God, love of my neighbor, love of my wife, of my husband—talked endlessly about love, they have no love in their hearts. If they had love in their hearts there would be a different kind of education, a different kind of business, a different world.

Collected Works, vol. XVII, pp. 261-2
Banaras, India, December 10, 1967

If we change in our relationship, society changes

Circumstances can be controlled by us, because we have created the circumstances. Society is the product of relationship, of yours and mine together. If we change in our relationship, society changes; merely to rely on legislation, on compulsion, for the transformation of outward society, while remaining inwardly corrupt, while continuing inwardly to seek power, position, domination, is to destroy the outward, however carefully and scientifically built. That which is inward is always overcoming the outward.

What causes war—religious, political or economic? Obviously belief, either in nationalism, in an ideology, or in a particular dogma. If we had no belief but goodwill, love and consideration between us, then there would be no wars. But we are fed on beliefs, ideas and dogmas and therefore we breed discontent. The present crisis is of an exceptional nature and we as human beings must either pursue the path of constant conflict and continuous wars, which are the result of our everyday action, or else see the causes of war and turn our back upon them.

Obviously what causes war is the desire for power, position, prestige, money; also the disease called nationalism, the worship of a flag, and the disease of organized religion, the worship of a dogma. All these are the causes of war; if you as an individual belong to any of the organized religions, if you are greedy for power, if you are envious, you are bound to produce a society which will result in destruction. So again it depends upon you and not on the leaders—not on so-called statesmen and all the rest of them. It depends upon you and me but we do not seem to realize that. If once we really felt the responsibility of our own actions, how quickly we could bring to an end all these wars, this appalling misery! But you see, we are indifferent. We have three meals a day, we have our jobs, we have our bank accounts, big or little, and we say, "For God's sake, don't disturb us, leave us alone". The higher up we are, the more we want security, permanency, tranquillity, the more we want to be left alone, to maintain things fixed as they are; but they cannot be maintained as they are, because there is nothing to maintain. Everything is disintegrating. We do not want to face these things, we do not want to face the fact that you and I are responsible for wars. You and I may talk about peace, have conferences, sit round a table and discuss, but inwardly, psychologically, we want power, position, we are motivated by greed. We intrigue, we are nationalistic, we are bound by beliefs, by dogmas, for which we are willing to die and destroy each other. Do you think such men, you and I, can have peace in the world? To have peace, we must be peaceful; to live peacefully means not to create antagonism. Peace is not an ideal. To me, an ideal is merely an escape, an avoidance of *what is,* a contradiction of what is. An ideal prevents direct action upon what is. To have peace, we will have to love, we will have to begin not to live an ideal life but to see things as they are and act upon them, transform them. As long as each one of us is seeking psychological security, the physiological security we need—food, clothing and shelter—is destroyed. We are seeking psychological security, which does not exist; and we seek it, if we can, through power, through position, through titles, names—all of which is destroying physical security. This is an obvious fact, if you look at it.

To bring about peace in the world, to stop all wars, there must be a revolution in the individual, in you and me. Economic revolution without this inward revolution is meaningless, for hunger is the result of the maladjustment of economic conditions produced by our psychological states—greed, envy, ill-will and possessiveness. To put an end to sorrow, to hunger, to war, there must be a psychological revolution and few of us are willing to face that. We will discuss peace, plan legislation, create new leagues, the United Nations and so on and on; but we will not win peace because we will not give up our position, our authority, our money, our properties, our stupid lives. To rely on others is utterly futile; others cannot bring us peace. No leader is going to give us peace, no government, no army, no country. What will bring peace is inward transformation which will lead to outward action. Inward transformation is not isolation, is not a withdrawal from outward action. On the contrary, there can be right action only when there is right thinking and there is no right thinking when there is no self-knowledge. Without knowing yourself, there is no peace.

To put an end to outward war, you must begin to put an end to war in yourself. Some of you will nod your heads and say, "I agree", and go outside and do exactly the same as you have been doing for the last ten or twenty years. Your agreement is merely verbal and has no significance, for the world's miseries and wars are not going to be stopped by your casual assent. They will be stopped only when you realize the danger, when you realize your responsibility, when you do not leave it to somebody else. If you realize the suffering, if you see the urgency of immediate action and do not postpone, then you will transform yourself; peace will come only when you yourself are peaceful, when you yourself are at peace with your neighbour.

The First and Last Freedom, pp. 183-185

A nation is the glorification of the self

Question: Don't you think there are peace-loving nations and aggressive nations?

Krishnamurti: No. The term *nation* is separative, exclusive and so the cause of contention and wars. There is no peace-loving nation; all are aggressive, dominant, tyrannical. As long as it remains a separate unit, apart from others, taking pride in segregation, in patriotism, in the race, it breeds untold misery for itself and for others. You may not have peace and yet be exclusive. You may not have economic and social, national and racial frontiers without inviting enmity and jealousy, fear and suspicion. You may not have plenty while others starve, without inviting violence. We are not separate, we are human beings in common relationship. Your sorrow is the sorrow of another—by killing another you are destroying yourself, by hating another you suffer, for you are the other. Goodwill and brotherliness are not achieved through separate and exclusive nationalities and frontiers; they must be set aside to bring peace and hope for man.

And besides, why do you identify yourself with any nation, with any group, or with any ideology? Is it not to protect your small self, to feed your petty and death-dealing vanities, sustain your own glory? What pride is there in the self which brings wars and misery, conflict and confusion? A nation is the glorification of the self and so the breeder of strife and sorrow.

Collected Works, vol. III, p. 227
Ojai, California, June 25, 1944

The unity of man is what matters, not one country against another country

Comment: War is the process of history.

Krishnamurti: Yes, madam, I know all this. India was overrun by the Chinese, and when we talked on this subject in India, they said, "What are you talking about? We are being attacked; therefore we must defend. An army is necessary." We are back again. The movement of hate, of war, will go on unless all of us see that hate cannot possibly end through hate, through defence. If we went and talked to the Vietnamese about not hating, they would throw us in the river or shoot us because they would think we were pacifists. That is what we mean when we say that there must be a total revolution in the mind so that we are no longer Christians, Buddhists, Catholics, communists, Americans, Hindus, Germans, and Italians—we are human beings. The unity of man is what matters, not one country against another country.

Collected Works, vol. XVI, pp. 224-5
Saanen, Switzerland, July 19, 1966

To have peace, the mind must be totally unconditioned

Your own mind is conditioned, and it is this conditioning that is really preventing peace, that is creating war, destruction, and misery. Unless you resolve your conditioning completely, there will be no real peace in the world; there will be the peace of politicians between two immense powers, which is terror. To have peace, the mind must be totally unconditioned. One must realize that, but not superficially, not as insurance for your security, or for your bank account. Peace is a state of mind; it is not the development of monstrous means of destroying each other and then maintaining peace through terror. I do not mean that. To have real peace in the world is to be able to live happily, creatively, without any sense of fear, without being secure in any thought, in any particular way of life. To have such peace, surely the mind must be totally free from all conditioning, either externally imposed or inwardly cultivated.

Collected Works, vol. VIII, pp. 218-9
New York, May 23, 1954

A stone may alter the course of a river

The prevention of this ever increasing destruction and horror depends on each one of us, not on any organization or planning, not on any ideology, not on the inventions of greater instruments of destruction, not on any leader but on each one of us. Do not think that wars cannot be stopped by so humble and lowly a beginning—a stone may alter the course of a river—to go far you must begin near. To understand the world chaos and misery, you must comprehend your own confusion and sorrow, for out of these come the magnified issues of the world. To understand yourself there must be constant meditative awareness which will bring to the surface the causes of violence and hate, greed and ambition, and by studying them without identification, thought will transcend them. For none can lead you to peace save yourself; there is no leader, no system that can bring war, exploitation, oppression to an end save yourself. Only by your thoughtfulness, by your compassion, by your awakened understanding can there be established good will and peace.

Collected Works, vol. III, pp. 242-3
Ojai, California, July 16, 1944

VI.   Education and World Peace

To discover what part education can play in the present world crisis, we should understand how that crisis has come into being. It is obviously the result of wrong values in our relationship to people, to property and to ideas. If our relationship with others is based on self-aggrandizement, and our relationship to property is acquisitive, the structure of society is bound to be competitive and self-isolating. If in our relationship with ideas we justify one ideology in opposition to another, mutual distrust and ill-will are the inevitable results.

Another cause of the present chaos is dependence on authority, on leaders, whether in daily life, in the small school or in the university. Leaders and their authority are deteriorating factors in any culture. When we follow another there is no understanding, but only fear and conformity, eventually leading to the cruelty of the totalitarian State and the dogmatism of organized religion.

To rely on governments, to look to organizations and authorities for that peace which must begin with the understanding of ourselves, is to create further and still greater conflict; and there can be no lasting happiness as long as we accept a social order in which there is endless strife and antagonism between man and man. If we want to change existing conditions, we must first transform ourselves, which means that we must become aware of our own actions, thoughts and feelings in everyday life.

But we do not really want peace, we do not want to put an end to exploitation. We will not allow our greed to be interfered with, or the foundations of our present social structure to be altered; we want things to continue as they are with only superficial modifications, and so the powerful, the cunning inevitably rule our lives.

Peace is not achieved through any ideology, it does not depend on legislation; it comes only when we as individuals begin to understand our own psychological process. If we avoid the responsibility of acting individually and wait for some new system to establish peace, we shall merely become the slaves of that system.

When governments, dictators, big business and the clerically powerful begin to see that this increasing antagonism between men only leads to indiscriminate destruction and is therefore no longer profitable, they may force us, through legislation and other means of compulsion, to suppress our personal cravings and ambitions and to co-operate for the well-being of mankind. just as we are now educated and encouraged to be competitive and ruthless, so then we shall be compelled to respect one another and to work for the world as a whole.

And even though we may all be well fed, clothed and sheltered, we shall not be free of our conflicts and antagonisms, which will merely have shifted to another plane, where they will be still more diabolical and devastating. The only moral or righteous action is voluntary, and understanding alone can bring peace and happiness to man.

Beliefs, ideologies and organized religions are setting us against our neighbours; there is conflict, not only among different societies, but among groups within the same society. We must realize that as long as we identify ourselves with a country, as long as we cling to security, as long as we are conditioned by dogmas, there will be strife and misery both within ourselves and in the world.

Then there is the whole question of patriotism. When do we feel patriotic? It is obviously not an everyday emotion. But we are sedulously encouraged to be patriotic through school-books, through newspapers and other channels of propaganda, which stimulate racial egotism by praising national heroes and telling us that our own country and way of life are better than others. This patriotic spirit feeds our vanity from childhood to old age.

The constantly repeated assertion that we belong to a certain political or religious group, that we are of this nation or of that, flatters our little egos, puffs them out like sails, until we are ready to kill or be killed for our country, race or ideology. It is all so stupid and unnatural. Surely, human beings are more important than national and ideological boundaries.

The separative spirit of nationalism is spreading like fire all over the world. Patriotism is cultivated and cleverly exploited by those who are seeking further expansion, wider powers, greater enrichment; and each one of us takes part in this process, for we also desire these things. Conquering other lands and other people provides new markets for goods as well as for political and religious ideologies.

One must look at all these expressions of violence and antagonism with an unprejudiced mind, that is, with a mind that does not identify itself with any country, race or ideology, but tries to find out what is true. There is great joy in seeing a thing clearly without being influenced by the notions and instructions of others, whether they be the government, the specialists or the very learned. Once we really see that patriotism is a hindrance to human happiness, we do not have to struggle against this false emotion in ourselves, it has gone from us forever.

Nationalism, the patriotic spirit, class and race consciousness, are all ways of the self, and therefore separative. After all, what is a nation but a group of individuals living together for economic and self-protective reasons ? Out of fear and acquisitive self defence arises the idea of "my country," with its boundaries and tariff walls, rendering brotherhood and the unity of man impossible.

The desire to gain and to hold, the longing to be identified with something greater than ourselves, creates the spirit of nationalism; and nationalism breeds war. In every country the government, encouraged by organized religion, is upholding nationalism and the separative spirit. Nationalism is a disease, and it can never bring about world unity. We can not attain health through disease, we must first free ourselves from the disease.

It is because we are nationalists, ready to defend our sovereign States, our beliefs and acquisitions, that we must be perpetually armed. Property and ideas have become more important to us than human life, so there is constant antagonism and violence between ourselves and others. By maintaining the sovereignty of our country, we are destroying our sons; by worshipping the State, which is but a projection of ourselves, we are sacrificing our children to our own gratification. Nationalism and sovereign governments are the causes and the instruments of war.

Our present social institutions cannot evolve into a world federation, for their very foundations are unsound. Parliaments and systems of education which uphold national sovereignty and emphasize the importance of the group will never bring war to an end. Every separate group of people, with its rulers and its ruled, is a source of war. As long as we do not fundamentally alter the present relationship between man and man, industry will inevitably lead to confusion and become an instrument of destruction and misery; as long as there is violence and tyranny, deceit and propaganda, the brotherhood of man cannot be realized.

Merely to educate people to be wonderful engineers, brilliant scientists, capable executives, able workmen, will never bring the oppressors and the oppressed together; and we can see that our present system of education, which sustains the many causes that breed enmity and hatred between human beings, has not prevented mass murder in the name of one's country or in the name of God.

Organized religions, with their temporal and spiritual authority, are equally incapable of bringing peace to man, for they also are the outcome of our ignorance and fear, of our make-believe and egotism.

Craving security here or in the hereafter, we create institutions and ideologies which guarantee that security; but the more we struggle for security, the less we shall have it. The desire to be secure only fosters division and increases antagonism. If we deeply feel and understand the truth of this, not merely verbally or intellectually, but with our whole being, then we shall begin to alter fundamentally our relationship with our fellow-men in the immediate world about us; and only then is there a possibility of achieving unity and brotherhood.

Most of us are consumed by all sorts of fears, and are greatly concerned about our own security. We hope that, by some miracle, wars will come to an end, all the while accusing other national groups of being the instigators of war, as they in turn blame us for the disaster. Although war is so obviously detrimental to society, we prepare for war and develop in the young the military spirit.

But has military training any place in education? It all depends on what kind of human beings we want our children to be. If we want them to be efficient killers, then military training is necessary. If we want to discipline them and regiment their minds, if our purpose is to make them nationalistic and therefore irresponsible to society as a whole, then military training is a good way to do it. If we like death and destruction, military training is obviously important. It is the function of generals to plan and carry on war; and if our intention is to have constant battle between ourselves and our neighbours, then by all means let us have more generals.

If we are living only to have endless strife within ourselves and with others, if our desire is to perpetuate bloodshed and misery, then there must be more soldiers, more politicians, more enmity— which is what is actually happening. Modern civilization is based on violence, and is therefore courting death. As long as we worship force, violence will be our way of life. But if we want peace, if we want right relationship among men, whether Christian or Hindu, Russian or American, if we want our children to be integrated human beings, then military training is an absolute hindrance, it is the wrong way to set about it.

One of the chief causes of hatred and strife is the belief that a particular class or race is superior to another. The child is neither class nor race conscious; it is the home or school environment, or both, which makes him feel separative. In himself he does not care whether his playmate is a Negro or a Jew, a Brahmin or a non-Brahmin; but the influence of the whole social structure is continually impinging on his mind, affecting and shaping it.

Here again the problem is not with the child but with the adults, who have created a senseless environment of separatism and false values.

What real basis is there for differentiating between human beings? Our bodies may be different in structure and colour, our faces may be dissimilar, but inside the skin we are very much alike: proud, ambitious, envious, violent, sexual, power-seeking and so on. Remove the label and we are very naked; but we do not want to face our nakedness, and so we insist on the label—which indicates how immature, how really infantile we are.

To enable the child to grow up free from prejudice, one has first to break down all prejudice within oneself, and then in one's environment—which means breaking down the structure of this thoughtless society which we have created. At home we may tell the child how absurd it is to be conscious of one's class or race, and he will probably agree with us; but when he goes to school and plays with other children, he becomes contaminated by the separative spirit. Or it may be the other way around: the home may be traditional, narrow, and the school's influence may be broader. In either case there is a constant battle between the home and the school environments, and the child is caught between the two.

To raise a child sanely, to help him to be perceptive so that he sees through these stupid prejudices, we have to be in close relationship with him. We have to talk things over and let him listen to intelligent conversation; we have to encourage the spirit of inquiry and discontent which is already in him, thereby helping him to discover for himself what is true and what is false.

It is constant inquiry, true dissatisfaction, that brings creative intelligence; but to keep inquiry and discontent awake is extremely arduous, and most people do not want their children to have this kind of intelligence, for it is very uncomfortable to live with someone who is constantly questioning accepted values.

All of us are discontented when we are young, but unfortunately our discontent soon fades away, smothered by our imitative tendencies and our worship of authority. As we grow older, we begin to crystallize, to be satisfied and apprehensive. We become executives, priests, bank clerks, factory managers, technicians, and slow decay sets in. Because we desire to maintain our positions, we support the destructive society which has placed us there and given us some measure of security.

Government control of education is a calamity. There is no hope of peace and order in the world as long as education is the handmaid of the state or of organized religion. Yet more and more governments are taking charge of the children and their future; and if it is not the government, then it is the religious organizations which seek to control education.

This conditioning of the child's mind to fit a particular ideology, whether political or religious, breeds enmity between man and man. In a competitive society we cannot have brotherhood, and no reform, no dictatorship, no educational method can bring it about.

As long as you remain a New Zealander and I a Hindu, it is absurd to talk about the unity of man. How can we get together as human beings if you in your country, and I in mine, retain our respective religious prejudices and economic ways? How can there be brotherhood as long as patriotism is separating man from man, and millions are restricted by depressed economic conditions while others are well off? How can there be human unity when beliefs divide us, when there is domination of one group by another, when the rich are powerful and the poor are seeking that same power, when there is maldistribution of land, when some are well fed and multitudes are starving?

One of our difficulties is that we are not really in earnest about these matters, because we do not want to be greatly disturbed. We prefer to alter things only in a manner advantageous to ourselves, and so we are not deeply concerned about our own emptiness and cruelty.

Can we ever attain peace through violence? Is peace to be achieved gradually, through a slow process of time? Surely, love is not a matter of training or of time. The last two wars were fought for democracy, I believe; and now we are preparing for a still greater and more destructive war, and people are less free. But what would happen if we were to put aside such obvious hindrances to understanding as authority, belief, nationalism and the whole hierarchical spirit? We would be people without authority, human beings in direct relationship with one another—and then, perhaps, there would be love and compassion.

What is essential in education, as in every other field, is to have people who are understanding and affectionate, whose hearts are not filled with empty phrases, with the things of the mind.

If life is meant to be lived happily, with thought, with care, with affection, then it is very important to understand ourselves; and if we wish to build a truly enlightened society, we must have educators who understand the ways of integration and who are therefore capable of imparting that understanding to the child.

Such educators would be a danger to the present structure of society. But we do not really want to build an enlightened society; and any teacher who, perceiving the full implications of peace, began to point out the true significance of nationalism and the stupidity of war, would soon lose his position. Knowing this, most teachers compromise, and thereby help to maintain the present system of exploitation and violence.

Surely, to discover truth, there must be freedom from strife, both within ourselves and with our neighbours. When we are not in conflict within ourselves, we are not in conflict outwardly. It is the inward strife which, projected outwardly, becomes the world conflict.

War is the spectacular and bloody projection of our everyday living. We precipitate war out of our daily lives; and without a transformation in ourselves, there are bound to be national and racial antagonisms, the childish quarrelling over ideologies, the multiplication of soldiers, the saluting of flags, and all the many brutalities that go to create organized murder.

Education throughout the world has failed, it has produced mounting destruction and misery. Governments are training the young to be the efficient soldiers and technicians they need; regimentation and prejudice are being cultivated and enforced. Taking these facts into consideration, we have to inquire into the meaning of existence and the significance and purpose of our lives. We have to discover the beneficent ways of creating a new environment; for environment can make the child a brute, an unfeeling specialist, or help him to become a sensitive, intelligent human being. We have to create a world government which is radically different, which is not based on nationalism, on ideologies, on force.

All this implies the understanding of our responsibility to one another in relationship; but to understand our responsibility, there must be love in our hearts, not mere learning or knowledge. The greater our love, the deeper will be its influence on society. But we are all brains and no heart; we cultivate the intellect and despise humility. If we really loved our children, we would want to save and protect them, we would not let them be sacrificed in wars.

I think we really want arms; we like the show of military power, the uniforms, the rituals, the drinks, the noise, the violence. Our everyday life is a reflection in miniature of this same brutal superficiality, and we are destroying one another through envy and thoughtlessness.

We want to be rich; and the richer we get, the more ruthless we become, even though we may contribute large sums to charity and education. Having robbed the victim, we return to him a little of the spoils, and this we call philanthropy. I do not think we realize what catastrophes we are preparing. Most of us live each day as rapidly and thoughtlessly as possible, and leave to the governments, to the cunning politicians, the direction of our lives.

All sovereign governments must prepare for war, and one's own government is no exception. To make its citizens efficient for war, to prepare them to perform their duties effectively, the government must obviously control and dominate them. They must be educated to act as machines, to be ruthlessly efficient. If the purpose and end of life is to destroy or be destroyed, then education *must* encourage ruthlessness; and I am not at all sure that that is not what we inwardly desire, for ruthlessness goes with the worship of success.

The sovereign State does not want its citizens to be free, to think for themselves, and it controls them through propaganda, through distorted historical interpretations and so on. That is why education is becoming more and more a means of teaching *what* to think and not *how* to think. If we were to think independently of the prevailing political system, we would be dangerous; free institutions might turn out pacifists or people who think contrary to the existing regime.

Right education is obviously a danger to sovereign governments —and so it is prevented by crude or subtle means. Education and food in the hands of the few have become the means of controlling man; and governments, whether of the left or of the right, are unconcerned as long as we are efficient machines for turning out merchandise and bullets.

Now, the fact that this is happening the world over means that we who are the citizens and educators, and who are responsible for the existing governments, do not fundamentally care whether there is freedom or slavery, peace or war, well-being or misery for man. We want a little reform here and there, but most of us are afraid to tear down the present society and build a completely new structure, for this would require a radical transformation of ourselves.

On the other hand, there are those who seek to bring about a violent revolution. Having helped to build the existing social order with all its conflicts, confusion and misery, they now desire to organize a perfect society. But can any of us organize a perfect society when it is we who have brought into being the present one? To believe that peace can be achieved through violence is to sacrifice the present for a future ideal; and this seeking of a right end through wrong means is one of the causes of the present disaster.

The expansion and predominance of sensate values necessarily creates the poison of nationalism, of economic frontiers, sovereign governments and the patriotic spirit, all of which excludes man's co-operation with man and corrupts human relationship, which is society. Society is the relationship between you and another; and without deeply understanding this relationship, not at any one level, but integrally, as a total process, we are bound to create again the same kind of social structure, however superficially modified.

If we are to change radically our present human relationship, which has brought untold misery to the world, our only and immediate task is to transform ourselves through self-knowledge. So we come back to the central point, which is oneself; but we dodge that point and shift the responsibility onto governments, religions and ideologies. The government is what *we* are, religions and ideologies are but a projection of ourselves; and until *we* change fundamentally there can be neither right education nor a peaceful world.

Outward security for all can come only when there is love and intelligence; and since we have created a world of conflict and misery in which outward security is rapidly becoming impossible for anyone, does it not indicate the utter futility of past and present education? As parents and teachers it is our direct responsibility to break away from traditional thinking, and not merely rely on the experts and their findings. Efficiency in technique has given us a certain capacity to earn money, and that is why most of us are satisfied with the present social structure; but the true educator is concerned only with right living, right education, and right means of livelihood.

The more irresponsible we are in these matters, the more the State takes over all responsibility. We are confronted, not with a political or economic crisis, but with a crisis of human deterioration which no political party or economic system can avert.

Another and still greater disaster is approaching dangerously close, and most of us are doing nothing whatever about it. We go on day after day exactly as before; we do not want to strip away all our false values and begin anew. We want to do patchwork reform, which only leads to problems of still further reform. But the building is crumbling, the walls are giving way, and fire is destroying it. We must leave the building and start on new ground, with different foundations, different values.

We cannot discard technical knowledge, but we can become inwardly aware of our ugliness, of our ruthlessness, of our deceptions and dishonesty, our utter lack of love. Only by intelligently freeing ourselves from the spirit of nationalism, from envy and the thirst for power, can a new social order be established.

Peace is not to be achieved by patchwork reform, nor by a mere rearrangement of old ideas and superstitions. There can be peace only when we understand what lies beyond the superficial, and thereby stop this wave of destruction which has been unleashed by our own aggressiveness and fears; and only then will there be hope for our children and salvation for the world.

Education and the Significance of Life, pp. 67-82

VII. Can the Human Being Completely Change?

The future of man is at stake

It is important that you and the speaker establish a right relationship. He is not a guru. He is not going to inform you what to think, how to think, but together we are going to observe the activities of human beings right throughout the world, why they have become what they are.

We are going to look together why man has become what he is —cruel, destructive, violent, idealistic and, in the world of technology, doing astonishing things of which most of us are unaware; why after thousands of years of wars, shedding tears, a human being, through a long period of time, is actually behaving in this manner. Man has divided the world into nationalities; man has divided the world into the Catholic, the Protestant, the Hindu, the Muslim and so on—religiously. Where there is division as the Arab and the Jew, the Hindu and the Muslim, and so on, where there is division, there must be conflict. This is a natural law, which is what is actually taking place in the world. Why is there this division? Who has brought this about? Why has man become what he is in spite of great experience, in spite of great knowledge, in spite of vast technological advancement; why has he remained more or less what he has been for 40,000 years; why? Is it because our mind, our brain, is programmed, like a computer? The computer is programmed by the professionals and it can repeat perhaps much quicker, more rapidly, than man, giving infinite information. Is it that every human being in this world has been programmed to be a Bengali, to be a Muslim, to be a Hindu, and so on? Is your brain programmed, thinking in a conventional, narrow, limited way? Our brain within the skull is limited. But it has the capacity of extraordinary invention, extraordinary technological advancement. Perhaps most of us do not know what is actually going on in the biological world, in the technological world, in the world of warfare, because most of us are concerned with our daily living, with our own particular problems, with our own fulfilments. So, we generally forget the vast advancement humanity is making in one direction, in the technological world, and totally, completely, neglecting the psychological world, the world of human behaviour, the world of consciousness. What are the causes of all this? Why are human beings being programmed as Christians for 2,000 years, believing in certain doctrines, certain beliefs, seeking only one saviour, and the Muslim also being programmed for the last 1,000 or more years to believe in certain principles and call himself a Muslim, and the Hindu being programmed perhaps for the last three to five thousand years. So our brains are conditioned. Does one ever realize how our brain is acting, thinking, looking? Where there is limitation, there must be conflict.

Our brains are conditioned to be this or that, to behave in a certain manner, to enjoy, to suffer, to have a great burden of fear, uncertainty, confusion and the ultimate fear of death. We are conditioned to that and there is a whole group of people, professors, scholars, writers, including the communists with their guru Marx, who say that the human brain will always be conditioned; it can never be free; you can modify that conditioning by environmental influence, by law. It can always be modified, changed here and there, but actually the human brain can never be free. Please understand the implication of that. Therefore, the totalitarian governments are controlling human thought and not allowing them to think freely, and if they do, they are sent to the psychiatric ward, to concentration camps. It is most important to find out for yourself whether the human brain which has been conditioned through experience, through knowledge, whether that brain can ever be free, have no fear, no conditioning. Where there is conditioning, there must be conflict, because all conditioning is limited. Is this clear?

In talking over together, you are aware of your own thinking, your own reactions, your own responses, how they are limited, how they are conditioned, how you depend on past knowledge. You see how your life becomes very narrow, rather sloppy, confused, and there is the fear of insecurity. If one is aware of all one's own inward activities, one's thoughts, one's feelings, one's reactions, then you will find out for yourself how conditioned you are, how limited you are. When you recognise that fact, then you realize the consequences of that conditioning, that limitation. Wherever there is limitation as Hindu or Muslim, there must be conflict. Wherever there is a division between husband and wife, there must be conflict. And human beings throughout the world, after all this evolution, are still in conflict with each other.

Please consider all this because we are concerned with your life as a human being. And that life, our daily living, has become extraordinarily complex, extraordinarily dangerous, difficult, uncertain. The future of man is really at stake. This is not a threat, this is not a pessimistic point of view. The crisis is not only physical, but it is in our consciousness, in our being. So, talking over together, become aware of all this. In becoming aware, you begin to discover. You begin to find out for yourself how your life has become such pain, such anxiety, such uncertainty. If you are so aware, you can then proceed more deeply, but if you merely listen to the words, words have very little meaning. Words have certain significance, but if one lives in words, as most people do, in symbols, in myths, in romantic nonsense, then we make life more and more difficult, more and more dangerous, for each other. So, please listen to find out, to question, to doubt, so that your own brain becomes aware of itself. We are asking why human beings, who have developed the most marvellous technology the world has ever known, have remained more or less the same psychologically, inwardly, for the last 40,000 years. Inwardly, we have systems, we have ideals, we have all the so-called sacred books, but we have not radically brought about a change, a psychological revolution, and we are going to enquire into that—whether it is possible to bring about total mutation in the brain cells themselves.

We are talking about the radical change of human behaviour so that man is not self-centred as he is, which is causing such great destruction in the world. If one is aware, then we can begin to ask whether that conditioning can be totally changed so that man is completely free. Now, he thinks he is free to do what he likes. Each individual thinks he can do what he likes, all over the world, and his freedom is based on choice because he can choose where to live, what kind of work he can do, choose between this idea and that idea, this ideal or that ideal, change from one god to another god from one guru to another, from one philosopher to another. This capacity to choose brings in the concept of freedom, but in the totalitarian state there is no freedom; you can't do what you want to do. It is totally controlled. Choice is not freedom. Choice is merely moving in the same field from one corner to another. Is this clear? Our brain being limited, we are asking, is it possible for the brain to free itself so that there is no fear? Then there is right relationship with all the neighbours in the world.

Now we are going to enquire into the nature of our consciousness. Your consciousness is what you are—your belief, your ideals, your gods, your violence, fear, romantic concepts, your pleasure, your sorrow, and the fear of death and the everlasting question of man, which has been from time immemorial, whether there is something sacred beyond all this. That is your consciousness. That is what you are, You are not different from your consciousness. We are asking whether that content of consciousness can be transformed, can be totally changed.

First, your consciousness is not yours. Your consciousness is the consciousness of all humanity, because what you think, your beliefs, your sensations, your reactions, your pain, your sorrow, your insecurity, your gods, and so on, are shared by all humanity. Go to America, go to England, Europe or Russia, China, you will find human beings suffer everywhere. They are frightened of death, they have beliefs, they have ideals. They speak a particular language, but their thinking, their reactions, their responses, generally are shared by all human beings. This is a fact that you suffer, your neighbour suffers; that neighbour may be thousands of miles away, but he suffers. He is as insecure as you are. He may have a lot of money but inwardly there is insecurity. A rich man in America, or the man in power, all go through this pain, anxiety, loneliness, despair. So, your consciousness is not yours any more than your thinking. It is not an individual thinking. Thinking is common, is general, from the poorest man, the most uneducated, unsophisticated man in a little, tiny village to the most sophisticated brain—the great scientists; they all think. The thinking may be more complex, but thinking is general, shared by all human beings. Therefore, it is not your individual thinking. This is rather difficult to see and to recognise the truth of it, because we are so conditioned as individuals. All your religious books, whether Christian or Muslim or another, all sustain and nourish this idea, this concept of an individual. You have to question that. You have to find out the truth of the matter.

We are investigating together and we see that human consciousness is similar, is shared by all human beings. Therefore, there is no individual. He may be more educated than you, he may be taller, he may be shorter; outside he may be different, but inwardly he shares the ground of all humanity. This is a fact. But if you are frightened, if you are caught in the conditioning of being an individual, you will never understand the immensity and the extraordinary fact that you are the entire humanity. From that there is love, compassion, intelligence, but if you are merely conditioned to the idea that you are an individual, then you have endless complications because it is based on illusion, not on fact. The illusion may be of thousands of years, but it is still illusion. You are the result of your environment, you are the result of the language you speak, you are the result of the food you eat, the clothes, the climate, the tradition handed down from generation to generation—you are all that. You are the product of the society which you have created. Society is not different from you. Man has created the society, the society of greed, envy, hatred, brutality, violence, wars; he has created all that and he has also created the extraordinary world of technology. So, you are the world and the world is you. Your consciousness is not yours, it is the ground on which all human beings stand, all human beings think. So, you are actually not an individual. That is one of the realities, truth that one must understand.

Do not accept what the speaker is saying, but question your own isolation, because individual means isolation. To separate oneself from another is isolation, like nations isolate themselves as Indians and all the rest of it. And they think that in isolation there is security. There is no security in isolation. But the governments of the world, representing the humanity of each country, are maintaining this isolation, and therefore they are perpetuating wars. If you recognise the truth, the fact that you are not an individual, that inwardly there is no division, that we all share the same problems, then the problem is: Can you, as a human being representing all humanity, bring about a fundamental, psychological, revolution? You might ask 'If I, as a human being, change, will it affect in any way the rest of mankind? If I do change, if there is a change in a particular person, how will it affect the whole consciousness of mankind?' Please do put that question to yourself; even as a single isolated human being you are asking, 'If I change, what effect has it in the world?'

The question is, if you change fundamentally, you affect the whole consciousness of man. Napoleon affected the whole consciousness of Europe. Stalin affected the whole consciousness of Russia. The Christian saviour, he has affected the consciousness of the world, and the Hindus with their peculiar gods have affected the consciousness of the world. When you, as a human being, radically transform psychologically, that is, be free of fear, have right relationship with each other, end sorrow and so on, which is a radical transformation, then you affect the whole consciousness of man. It is not an individual affair. It is not a selfish affair. It is not individual salvation; it is the salvation of all human beings of which you are.

First, we must enquire what is relationship. Why is there, in human relationship with each other, such conflict, such misery, such intense sense of loneliness? From past history, from all the knowledge that has been acquired, studied, man has lived in conflict with each other. But relationship is existence: without relationship you cannot exist. In that existence there is conflict. Relationship is absolutely necessary. Life is relationship, action is relationship; what you think brings about relationship or destroys relationship. The hermit, the monk, the sanyasi—he may think he is separate, but he is related—related to the past, related to the environment, related to the man who brings him some grains, some food, some clothes. So life is relationship. We are going to explore together why human beings live in conflict with each other, why there is conflict between you and your husband, between the wife and the man. Because, where there is conflict in relationship, there is no love, there is no compassion, and there is no intelligence. Are you actually related? You may be related to a man, woman, sexually, but apart from that, are you related to anybody? Relation means non-isolation. That is, the man goes to the office every day of his life, to a factory, to some form of occupation, leaving the house at 8 o'clock, spends the whole day working, for 50, 60 years, and then dies. And there the man is ambitious, greedy, envious, struggling, competing; he comes home and the woman, the wife, is also competitive, jealous, anxious, going on in her own way. They may meet sexually, talk together, care somewhat, but they remain separate, like two railway lines never meeting. This is what we call relationship, which is an actuality. This is a fact of everyone's life, the perpetual division between two people, each holding on to his opinions, to his conclusions. The fact is, however intimate that relationship may be, there is always conflict, one dominating the other, one possessing the other, one jealous of the other. This is what we call relationship. Now, can that relationship which we know, be totally changed? Ask yourself this.

Why is there conflict between two human beings, whether they are highly educated or not at all educated? They may be great scientists, but they are ordinary human beings, like you and another —fighting, quarrelling, ambitious. Why does this state exist? Is it not because each person is concerned about himself? So he is isolating himself. In isolation you cannot have right relationship. You hear this, but you will not do anything about it because we fall into a habit, into a rut, into a groove, into a narrow little life, and we put up with it, however miserable, unhappy, quarrelsome, ugly, it is. So, please enquire, question, doubt, whether it is possible to live with another with complete harmony without any dissension, without any division. If you really, deeply, enquire, you will find that you have created an image about your wife, and she has created an image about you. Each has built an image about the other, a picture about the other. These two pictures, images, words, are in relationship with each other. Where there is an image about another, a picture about another, there must be conflict. I am sure you all have an image about the speaker. I am quite sure of it. Why? You don't know the speaker. You can never know the speaker, but you have created an image about him: that he is religious, non-religious, he is stupid, he is very clever, he is beautiful, he is this, he is that. And with that image you look at the person. The image is not the person. The image is the reputation, and reputations are easily created; the reputation may be good or bad. But the human brain, the thought, creates the image. The image is the conclusion, and we live by images and imagination. The making of pictures has no place in love. We don't love each other; we may hold hands, we may sleep together, we may do this and ten different things, but we have no love for each other. If you had that quality, that perfume of love, there would be no wars. There will be no Hindu and Muslim, Jew and Arab. But you listen to all this and you still remain with your images. You still wrangle with each other, quarrel with each other. Your life has become so extraordinarily meaningless.

I wonder how many of you realize that we are put together by thought. Your gods are put together by thought. All the rituals, all the dogmas, the philosophy, are all put together by thought, and thought is not sacred. Thought is always limited. Thought has created an image about you as the audience, about you as the wife and the husband, about you as the Indian and he as the American, and so on. It is these images which are unreal, which are dividing humanity. You should never call yourself an Indian, Russian or American; we are human beings. Then we should have no wars. We should have global government, global relationship, but you are not interested in all that. You hear all this, and if you don't change radically, you are bringing about destruction to the future generation. So, please give ear, give thought, attention, to what is going on outside you and also to what is going on inwardly, for the inward psyche conquers the outer environment. As you see it in Russia, we give such importance to the outer. We must have right society, right laws, feed the poor, be concerned about the poor, but the inward thought, inward feeling, inward isolation, is separating man from man, and you are responsible for this. Each one of you is responsible for this. Unless you change fundamentally, inwardly, the future is very dangerous. Unless you fundamentally bring about a change in your daily life, have right relationship with each other, live correctly, not be ambitious and so on, there is no possibility for the ending of conflict between human beings.

Mind Without Measure, pp. 33-41
Calcutta, India, November 20, 1982

My responsibility is not to have an image

Krishnamurti: What is the responsibility of a human being in relationship? Because relationship is life, relationship is the foundation of existence. Relationship is absolutely necessary, otherwise you cannot exist. Relationship means co-operation. Everything is involved in that one word. Relation means love, generosity, all that's implied. Now what is a human responsibility in relationship?

Professor Anderson: If we were genuinely and completely sharing then responsibility would be fully present.

K: Yes, but how does it express itself in relationship? Not only between you and me now, but between man and woman, with my neighbour, relationship to everything, to Nature. What's my relationship to Nature? Would I go and kill baby seals?

A: No.

K: Would I go and destroy human beings calling them enemies? Would I destroy Nature, everything which man is doing now? He is destroying the earth, the air, the sea, everything because he feels totally irresponsible.

A: He sees what is out there as something to operate on.

K: So I ask how does this responsibility show itself in my life? Suppose I am married, what is my responsibility? Am I related to my wife?

A: The record doesn't seem very good.

K: Not only record, the actuality. Am I related to my wife? Or am I related to my wife according to the image I make about her? And I am responsible for that image, do you follow, sir?

A: Yes, because my input has been continuous with respect to that image.

K: So I have no relationship with my wife if I have an image about her. Or if I have an image about myself when I want to be successful and all the rest of that business.

A: Since we were talking about now, being now, there ia a point of contact, I take it, between what you are saying and the phrase that you used in one of our earlier conversations, the betrayal of the present.

K: Absolutely. You see that is the whole point, sir. If I am related to you, I have no image about you, or you have no image about me, then we have relationship. We have no relationship if I have an image about myself or about you. Our images have a relationship, but in actuality we have no relationship. I might sleep with my wife but it is not a relationship. It is a physical contact, sensory excitement, nothing else. My responsibility is not to have an image.

I must stick to this because this is really quite important. Because go where you will there is no relationship between human beings, and that is the tragedy, and from that arises all our conflicts, violence, the whole business. So when there is this responsibility, the feeling of this responsibility, it translates itself in relationship. It doesn't matter with whom. There is a freedom from the known which is the image. And in that freedom, goodness flowers.

A: Goodness flowers.

K: And that is the beauty. Beauty is not an abstract thing, but it goes with goodness. Goodness in behaviour, goodness in conduct, goodness in action.

A: Sometimes while we have been talking I have started a sentence with 'if', and I have looked into your eyes and immediately I knew I had said the wrong thing. We are always 'iffing' it up.

K: 'Iffing' it up! I know, sir. We are always dealing with abstractions rather than with reality.

A: Immediately we 'if', a construction is out there which we endlessly talk about.

K: That's right.

A: And we get cleverer and cleverer about it and it has nothing to do with anything.

K: So how does this responsibility translate itself in human behaviour? You follow, sir?

A: There would be an end to violence.

K: Absolutely.

A: It wouldn't taper off.

K: You see what we have done, sir? We are violent human beings, sexually, morally, in every way we are violent human beings, and not being able to resolve it we have created an ideal of not being violent, which means there is the fact—violence—an abstraction from the fact which is non-fact, and we try to live the non-fact.

A: Yes, and immediately that produces conflict because it cannot be done.

K: Conflict, misery, confusion all that. Why does the mind do it? The mind does it because it doesn't know what to do with the fact of violence. Therefore in abstracting the idea of not being violent, it postpones action. I am trying not to be violent and in the mean time I am jolly well violent.

A: Yes.

K: And this is an escape from the fact. All abstractions are escape from the fact. So the mind does it because it is incapable of dealing with the fact or it doesn't want to deal with the fact or it is lazy and says, I will try and do it another day. All this is involved when it withdraws from the fact. Now in the same way the fact is our relationship is non-existent. I may say to my wife, I love you, etc., etc., but it's non-existent, because I have an image about her and she has an image about me. So we have lived on abstractions.

A: It occurs to me that the word 'fact' itself, which there have been no end of disquisitions about...

K: Oh yes, of course. The fact, 'what is', let's call it, 'what is'. You see, sir, this reveals a tremendous lot. When you feel responsible, feel responsible for the education of your children, not only yours, all children. Are you educating them to conform to society, are you educating them to merely acquire a job? Are you educating them to the continuity of what has been? Are you educating them to live in abstractions, as we are doing now? So what is your responsibility as a father, mother, it doesn't matter who you are, for the education of a human being? That's one problem. What is your responsibility, if you feel responsible, for human growth, human culture, human goodness? What's your responsibility to the Earth? It is a tremendous thing to feel responsible. And also, you see, with responsibility goes love, care, attention.

A: Yes, earlier I was going to ask you about care in relation to responsibility. Something that would flow immediately.

K: Naturally. You see that involves a great deal too because the mother depends on the child, and the child depends on the mother, or the father, or whatever it is. So that dependence is cultivated: not only between the father and the mother but dependence on a teacher, dependence on somebody to tell you what to do, dependence on your guru.

A: Yes, I follow.

K: Gradually the child, the man, is incapable of standing alone and therefore he says I must depend on my wife for my comfort, for my sex, for this, that, and the other thing, I am lost without her. And I am lost without my guru, without my teacher. It becomes so ridiculous. When the feeling of responsibility exists all this disappears. You are responsible for your behaviour, for the way you bring up your children, for the way you treat a dog, a neighbour, Nature, everything is in your hands. Therefore you have to become astonishingly careful about what you do. Careful, not, 'I must not do this and I must do that'. Care, that means affection, that means consideration, diligence. All that goes with responsibility, which present-day society totally denies. That's what the various gurus that are imported into the West are doing, creating such mischief making those people unfortunate, thoughtless people, who want excitement, join them, to do all kinds of ridiculous nonsensical things.

So, we come back: freedom implies responsibility. And therefore freedom, responsibility means care, diligence, not negligence.

A Wholly Different Way of Living, pp. 57-61
San Diego, California, February 19, 1974
4th Conversation with Dr. Allan W. Anderson

Unless there is a change, there will always be war

So our question is: How can a brain as well as the mind—that is, the total human being—physiologically, neurologically, completely change? How can the human being completely change? Such a change is necessary—one sees that. And unless there is a change, there will always be war—one nation against another, one nationality against another, all that terrible brutality of war, your country against another country, the linguistic differences, the economic differences, the social differences, the moral differences and the everlasting battle, outward and inward. There must be change. Now, how is one to bring it about?

Please see the extraordinary complexity of this question, what is involved in it. Man has tried so many ways—gone away to the monasteries, renounced the world and taken *sannyasas,* gone into the woods and meditated, fasted, become a celibate, has done everything that he could possibly imagine, has mesmerized himself, has forced himself, has examined, analysed his consciousness, the conscious and the unconscious—he has done everything to bring about a radical revolution within himself. And he has been ruthless therefore in himself, not only as an individual, but as a human being—the two are entirely different. The individual is a local entity: a Parsi, a Buddhist, a Muslim, and so on. The individual is conditioned by the environment. But the human being is beyond that; he is concerned with the total man—not about his country, the linguistic differences, his little wars and quarrels, his petty little gods, and so on—he is concerned with the whole state of man, his conflict, his despair. When you see the whole, then you can understand the particular. But the particular cannot possibly understand the whole. So, for the constantly introspective individual, inquiry has no meaning at all because he is still concerned with the pattern of his own existence, conditioned by society—in which is included religion and all the rest of it. Whereas man—as a human being who has lived for two million years—has suffered, has thought, has inquired, has borne, whether in Russia, in China, in America, or here.

And man, the human being, has done everything to bring about a radical change; and yet, fundamentally, man has not changed at all. We are what we have been for two million years! The animal is very strong in us. The animal with all its greed, envy, ambition, anger, ruthlessness still exists deep down in our hearts and mind. And we have through religion, through culture, through civilization, polished the outer; we have better manners—perhaps a few of us have better manners. We know a little more. Technologically we have gone very far. We can discuss Western and Eastern philosophy, literature; we can travel all over the world. But inwardly, deep down, the roots are very firmly embedded.

Seeing all this, how is one—you as a human being and I as a human being—how are we to change? Certainly not through tears, certainly not through intellection, not through following an ideological utopia, not through external tyranny, nor through self-imposed tyranny. So one discards all this, and I hope you have also discarded all this. Do you understand? To discard one's nationality;

to discard one's gods, one's traditions, one's beliefs; to discard all the things that we have been brought up to believe in—to discard all this is a very difficult thing to do. We may intellectually agree, but deep down in the unconscious there is the insistence on the importance of the past to which we cling.

Collected Works, vol. XVI, pp. 48-9
Bombay, February 16, 1966

It is not a matter of saving your own particular little soul

It is not a revolution within oneself as an individual that we are talking about—a matter of saving your own particular little soul—but a revolution within oneself as a human being totally related to all other human beings. We may consciously separate ourselves into petty, little individualities, but deep down, unconsciously, we are the inherited human experience of all time; and mere superficial changes on the economic or social level, though they may provide a little more comfort and convenience, are not productive of a new society. We are concerned, not only with the human being's transformation of his total nature, but also with bringing about a different society, a good society; and a good society is not possible if there are no good human beings.

Collected Works, vol. XV, p. 203
Saanen, Switzerland, July 18, 1965

Cultivating your back yard isn't going to do very much

Question: What effect does a revolution in the mind of a single person have on the whole human race?

Krishnamurti: As we explained before, the individual is the local entity, the American, the Russian, the Indian—the local, conditioned, modern entity. The human being is much older. You are asking, if there is a mutation in the human mind, whether it will affect the whole consciousness, not only of the individual, but of man.

There are several things involved in this question: first, how to change society. You see that society must be changed, but how? And is it possible? Realizing the vested interests of the politicians, of the army, of the priests, of the business men, is it possible? You are society, psychologically. You have created this society; you are part of it. The psychological structure of society is what you have psychologically created. It is not something different from you. You have conflict; your life, your daily existence is a battlefield; and the battlefield in Vietnam is the extension of your daily life. You say, "I want to change all that." Can it be changed, or should you be concerned with the total human being, the human being who is ten thousand or two million or whatever years old? If there can be mutation there, then everything will come right. Merely changing a local entity, the individual, is not going to affect it a very great deal. Cultivating your back yard isn't going to do very much. But when you are concerned with the total man, then in that mutation of the psyche, perhaps the mutation will affect society.

Collected Works, vol. XVII, p. 46
New York, October 7, 1966

It is because we function as localized entities that we are destroying ourselves

Comment: Sir, what you are really telling us is to cultivate a private state of mind. I stress the word private. *But the point is that you do have to live in the material world. Surely the active world can destroy our private state of mind.*

Krishnamurti: Sir, I am not talking of the private mind at all. Our minds are the result of the totality of the human mind. We are the result of the society in which we live. This society has been created by each one of us. So the many is the 'me' and the 'me' is the many. There is no division between me and the many. I am the result of all that. However, I think we should differentiate between the individual and the human being. The individual is the localized entity, the Englishman, the Indian, the American, and so on, localized, conditioned by the locality, the culture, the climate, the food, the clothes. The human being is conditioned on a much larger scale. He belongs to the whole world. Our sufferings, anxieties, and fears are the same as in India, as those of an Indian who goes through terrible states, just like everyone else all over the world. If we understand that, then the private cultivation of one's own mind also disappears. We are concerned with the total structure of the human mind, not our minds, our little backyards. That's nothing. Our little backyards are as filthy as any other backyard, or as clean as any other little back yard.

My action then is not outside the world but in the world, all the time I'm here. What I'm doing as a human being, going to the office, living with my family, I'm aware of, not as a private individual, but as a human being. When I'm aware of that as a human being, surely I'm affecting the whole of the human mind. It is because we function as localized entities that we are destroying ourselves. Sir, at the present time India is going through a terrible period of starvation and hardships. The question is not an Indian question; it is a human question. The politicians won't see that. They want to keep their localities intact, with their sovereign states, their power, their position, their prestige. They won't solve the problem that way. It is a human problem; it is a world problem. We have to deal with it as a whole world, not Indians or communists or Americans or Englishmen giving food or not giving food. Action as a human being is entirely different from the action of a localized entity. The localized entity creates more harm, creates misery, as does the human being who is still caught in the human or the animalistic struggle. Only the human being who has understood this whole structure, its anxieties and its agonies, can bring about a totally different kind of action.

Collected Works, vol. XVI, p. 150
London, May 7, 1966

Is it possible to live a life that is completely free from all psychological conflict?

Is it possible for there to be no conflict at all, right through one's life? Traditionally, one accepts that there must be this conflict, this struggle, this everlasting fight, not only physiologically in order to survive, but psychologically in desire and fear, like and dislike, and so on. To live without conflict is to live a life without any effort, a life in which there is peace. Man has lived, centuries upon centuries, a life of battle, conflict, both outwardly and inwardly; a constant struggle to achieve and fear of losing, dropping back. One may talk endlessly about peace, but there will be no peace as long as one is conditioned to the acceptance of conflict. If one says it is possible to live in peace, then it is just an idea and therefore valueless. And if one says it is not possible, then one blocks any investigation.

Go into it psychologically first; it is more important than physiologically. If one understands very deeply the nature and the structure of conflict psychologically and perhaps ends it there, then one may be able to deal with the physiological factor. But if one is only concerned with the physiological, biological factor, to survive, then one probably will not be able to do it at all.

Why is there this conflict, psychologically? From ancient times, both socially and religiously, there has been a division between the good and the bad. Is there really this division at all—or is there only "what is", without its opposite? Suppose there is anger; that is the fact, that is "what is", but "I will not be angry" is an idea, not a fact.

One never questions this division, one accepts it because one is traditional by habit, not wanting anything new. But there is a further factor; there is a division between the observer and the observed. When one looks at a mountain, one looks at it as an observer and one calls it a mountain. The word is not the thing. The word "mountain" is not the mountain, but to oneself the word is very important; when one looks, instantly there is the response, "that is a mountain". Now, can one look at the thing called "mountain", without the word, because the word is a factor of division? When one says "My wife," the word "my" creates division. The word, the name, is part of thought. When one looks at a man or a woman, a mountain or a tree, whatever it is, division takes place when thought, the name, the memory, comes into being.

Can one observe without the observer, who is the essence of all the memories, experiences, reactions and so on, which are from the past? If one looks at something without the word and the past memories, then one looks without the observer. When one does that, there is only the observed and there is no division and no conflict, psychologically. Can one look at one's wife or one's nearest intimate friend without the name, the word and all the experiences that one has gathered in that relationship? When one so looks one is looking at her or him for the first time.

Is it possible to live a life that is completely free from all psychological conflict? One has observed the fact, it will do everything if one lets the fact alone. As long as there is division between the image-making observer, and the fact—which is no image but only fact—there must be everlasting conflict. That is a law. That conflict can be ended.

When there is an ending of psychological conflict—which is part of suffering—then how does that apply to one's livelihood, how does that apply in one's relationship with others? How does that ending of psychological struggle, with all its conflicts, pain, anxiety, fear, how does that apply to one's daily living—one's daily going to the office etc. etc? If it is a fact that one has ended psychological conflict, then how will one live a life without conflict outwardly? When there is no conflict inside, there is no conflict outside, because there is no division between the inner and the outer. It is like the ebb and flow of the sea. It is an absolute, irrevocable fact, which nobody can touch, it is inviolate. So, if that is so, then what shall one do to earn a livelihood? Because there is no conflict, therefore there is no ambition. Because there is no conflict, there is no desire to be something. Because inwardly there is something absolute which is inviolate, which cannot be touched, which cannot be damaged, then one does not depend psychologically on another; therefore there is no conformity, no imitation. So, not having all that, one is no longer heavily conditioned to success and failure in the world of money, position, prestige, which implies the denial of "what is" and the acceptance of "what should be".

Because one denies "what is" and creates the ideal of "what should be" there is conflict. But to observe what actually is, means one has no opposite, only "what is". If you observe violence and use the word "violence" there is already conflict, the very word is already warped: there are people who approve of violence and people who do not. The whole philosophy of non-violence is warped, both politically and religiously. There is violence and its opposite, non-violence. The opposite exists because you know violence. The opposite has its root in violence. One thinks that by having an opposite, by some extraordinary method or means, one will get rid of "what is".

Now, can one put away the opposite and just look at violence, the fact? The non-violence is not a fact. Non-violence is an idea, a concept, a conclusion. The fact is violence—that one is angry; that one hates somebody; that one wants to hurt people; that one is jealous; all that is the implication of violence, that is the fact. Now, can one observe that fact without introducing its opposite? For then one has the energy—which was being wasted in trying to achieve the opposite—to observe "what is". In that observation there is no conflict.

So, what will a man do who has understood this extraordinary complex existence based on violence, conflict, struggle, a man who is actually free of it, not theoretically, but actually free? Which means, no conflict. What shall he do in the world? Will one ask this question if one is inwardly, psychologically, completely free from conflict? Obviously not. It is only the man in conflict who says: "If there is no conflict, I will be at an end, I will be destroyed by society because society is based on conflict."

If one is aware of one's consciousness, what is one? If one is aware, one will see that one's consciousness is—in its absolute sense —in total disorder. It is contradictory, saying one thing, doing something else, always wanting something. The total movement is within an area which is confined and without space and in that little space there is disorder.

Is one different from one's consciousness? Or is one that consciousness? One is that consciousness. Then is one aware that one is in total disorder? Ultimately that disorder leads to neurosis, obviously—and all the specialists in modern society such as psychoanalysts, psychotherapists and so on. But inwardly, is one in order? Or is there disorder? Can one observe this fact? And what takes place when one observes choicelessly—which means without any distortion? Where there is disorder, there must be conflict. Where there is absolute order there is no conflict. And there is an absolute order, not relative order. That can only come about naturally, easily, without any conflict, when one is aware of oneself as a consciousness, aware of the confusion, the turmoil, the contradiction, outwardly and inwardly observing without any distortion. Then out of that comes naturally, sweetly, easily, an order which is irrevocable.

The Wholeness of Life, 203-6
Ojai, California, April 3, 1977

VIII. How Does the Free Mind
Live in This World?

Knowing what the world is, which each one of us has created, with all its fragmentation and division, with its brutalities, chicanery, deceptions, violence and wars and all the horrors that are going on, we have two central problems. First, is it possible to turn our back on this world—that is, to turn away from the culture, the civilization, all that man has put together throughout the centuries, and free the mind from that conditioning? That is one issue. Secondly, is it possible in the very process of unconditioning the mind to live in this world, yet not of it, not be involved in it?

I do not know if you have considered how serious this is. It is not an entertainment, something that one seeks out of pleasure, or out of despair, but rather, being aware of the whole situation, the various intricacies in the world movement, historically, outwardly and inwardly, these questions are a matter of urgent concern. Man has destroyed nature, exterminated certain species of animals and birds. He has created the most beautiful cathedrals, mosques and temples, great literature, music, painting. And that is part of our culture, the beauty, the ugliness, the cruelty, the immense destruction of man by man. That is part of our civilization, of which we are part. I do not know if you really fully realize what is involved in all this, economically, socially, religiously. If you have examined it in some depth, you must be concerned with whether the structure can be changed, the structure that has created this world; you must have asked what has brought about this structure, and whether by merely changing the structure man will be changed? This has been one of the theories of the world: change the outer conditions, then man will be changed inwardly—that has always been one of the arguments. But you see that it doesn't work that way. So it is man who has to change and thereby change the structure.

Now can the mind, your mind, be free from this culture? And what does it mean to be free from culture? Is it a matter of analysis? Is it a matter of time? Is it a matter of more rational, logical conclusions of thought? Or is it a non-movement of thought? Please go into this with me a little bit. It may be somewhat difficult —you may not be used to this kind of thinking, you may not have thought about it at all. So please have a little patience and thereby share together this extraordinary question. Can this conditioning of the mind, which has been brought about through time, experience and knowledge, be dissolved by analysis? That is one point.

Analysis, the very word means to break up. And through fragmentation we hope to understand and dissolve the complex problem of conditioning, both at the conscious and the unconscious level. Can this be done through analysis, between the analyser and the analysed, taking months, years? All that involves time and by that time you will be dead! I can analyse myself very, very carefully, step by step, investigate the cause, the effect, the effect becoming the cause, which is the chain in which analysis is caught. Can the mind analyse itself and dissolve all its peculiarities, violence, superstitions, the various contradictions, and thereby bring about a total harmony?

As we said, analysis implies time, and what is time? Time is both a physical and a psychological movement—physically, a movement from here to there, psychologically a movement from 'what is' to 'what should be', transforming 'what is' through an ideology, which is a movement in time. Right? Please, we are sharing this question together, you are not just listening to me; we are travelling together, investigating, together finding out what is true. It is not for you to accept what the speaker is saying; that has no value whatsoever, neither verbally nor in reality. What has reality is when we, through investigation, through observation, through very careful awareness, share that which we discover for ourselves. That has validity; it has substance, meaning. There is no significance in merely listening to a series of words and translating these into ideas, and then putting these ideas into action.

So, as we are saying, time is movement. Physically moving from here to there takes time. Psychologically it is also a movement, from 'what is' and changing to 'what should be'. 'What is', which is the result of the past, is a movement in time to the present, and 'what should be' is a movement into the future. The whole movement is time. Right? And thought is always a process in time, for thought is the response of memory, which is the past, based on knowledge which is also the past, and according to that conditioning it reacts, which is a movement. So thought is a movement in time. And analysis is a movement in time, the movement of thought examining itself. And we are conditioned to analyse. You will see, if you go into it deeply, that that is our conditioning. We never see that the cause becomes the effect, and the effect becomes the cause. That is a movement in time. Analysis does not free the mind, which is the result of time.

I wonder if you see this? It is fairly simple if you observe it in yourself. I am angry. I analyse the cause, and in the process of analysis I come to a conclusion, which is the effect. And that conclusion becomes the cause to the next effect. All that is a movement of thought in time. Thought *is* time. And thought has built this conditioning. All our culture is the result of thought, as feeling, physical responses and so on. So analysis cannot possibly resolve the conditioning of the human mind. I hope it is clear—not the verbal statement, but the truth of it, the actual fact, nor the assertion or the repetition of a statement, that analysis will not free the mind. That has no value.

So the mind, seeing the falseness of analysis, discovers the truth that analysis does not free the mind—that is, it discovers the truth *in* the false. Now, analysis involves not only the conscious mind but also the deep layers of the unconscious, which is also the result of time. This division between the conscious and the unconscious is artificial. Consciousness is total. We may divide it, we may break it up to examine it, but it is a total movement within the field of time. And the unconscious looses its importance when you are able to look at the whole of consciousness and its content. You understand? We look at ourselves fragmentarily. We look at ourselves through the action of thought.

Look, sirs, my consciousness is a total movement. It can be broken up as the conscious and the unconscious, as action and inaction, as greed, envy, non-envy; it is a totality, a total movement which can be fragmented only in order to examine it. And I see that an examination of fragments doesn't bring about a comprehension of the whole. Right? What is needed is to be aware of the whole, not merely of the fragments. To be aware of the whole movement of consciousness, which is in the area of time. Can thought, can I, as thought, explore this consciousness? You see, what I am trying to say is this: personally, I have never analysed myself at all. What has taken place is observation, and in that very observation the total is revealed because there is no intention of going beyond 'what is'. Going beyond 'what is' is the movement of time. Is that fairly clear?

So I see clearly that the mind can, without analysis, discover, observe, the total movement of consciousness. That is one point. What we are concerned with is whether the mind can free itself from its conditioning. I see it cannot free itself from its conditioning through analysis as that involves time, and to dissolve time through time is not possible. Then can thought dissolve itself? Can thought transform, free the mind from its conditioning? Now please listen to this. Thought is movement in time; thought is movement and therefore time. And the examination by thought of the movement of the conditioning is still within the field of time, therefore thought cannot possibly resolve the conditioning because it is thought as knowledge, experience, memory, that has brought about this civilization in which the mind has been educated. That is clear. So thought cannot resolve it. Analysis cannot. Then what have you left? You understand? We have used thought as a means of conquering, destroying, changing, analysing, overcoming. And I see that thought cannot possibly bring freedom to the mind. Thought is movement. Thus *non-movement* is freedom from time. Right? Non-movement of thought is a state in which the mind is free from time. Now, I'll go into this; you will see it.

The conditioning of civilization, culture, has emphasized that I must be competitive, has taught me to be violent, or, rather, encouraged me to be more violent. So the mind is violent; that is 'what is'. Can the mind be free of violence, which is 'what is', without the movement of thought? You understand my question? I am violent and thought says, 'Overcome that violence, control that violence, utilize that violence,' thus encouraging or controlling, shaping that violence for its own purposes. That is what we are doing all the time. So thought, being a movement, is continuously acting upon 'what is', which is also the result of time and thought. Right? Now can thought have no movement at all and only the 'what is' remains without any interference of thought? Look, sirs, I am violent, I know all the causes, how violence has come about. That is fairly clear, it is part of the culture, encouraged by the economic situation, education and so on. I am violent, that is 'what is'. Can the mind look at 'what is' without any movement? Any movement is time. So can the mind observe that violence with non-thought, that is, without time?

Have you at least understood my question? My conditioning says, 'Use thought to control violence, to shape it, to get rid of it, to struggle against it; it is ugly to be violent, human beings should be peaceful.' So it provides all the reasons, justifications, condemnations, which are all movements of thought, and thought is time, and movement is time. Yet there is only the fact that this human being is violent. So far that is clear.

Can the mind look at 'what is' without any movement? The 'what is' is violence. Now, I have used a word to indicate a feeling which I have named 'violence', and that word with its meaning I have already used before. So I am recognizing the feeling in terms of the old. Whenever I recognize something it must be the old. So 'what is' is the result of thought. Now the mind meets without movement, which means without time, that which has been put together by thought, which I have called 'violence'. So when non-movement meets thought, which is the movement of time, then what takes place? You are following?

Look, sirs, my son dies; I suffer a great deal for various reasons, loneliness, despair and so on. Then thought comes along and says, 'I must overcome it'. The 'what is' is suffering, and the movement of thought is time. The mind meets that suffering and tries to do something about it, to escape from it, seeks comfort in seances, in mediums, in beliefs; it goes through all that process, which is all a movement of time as thought. Now, in meeting that suffering without any movement, what takes place? Have you ever tried this? If you have, you will see that the non-movement completely transforms the movements of time, and that which we call suffering is time. That means suffering doesn't leave a mark on the mind at all because non-movement is timeless, and that cannot possibly touch that which is not of itself.

So the mind is conditioned through culture, through environment, through knowledge, through experience—all of which is the movement of time, and thought is also a movement of time. Thus thought cannot possibly transform or free the mind from its conditioning, just as analysis cannot. The question is, can the mind observe this conditioning, this educated entity, without any movement? If you do it, then you will see that all sense of control, imitation, conformity, totally disappears.

Now the next question is: can the mind, freeing itself from its conditioning which is the result of time, live in this world, which has been brought about by the intricacies of thought as movement, in time? Right? My question is: can a human being, freeing himself from his conditioning—freeing doesn't mean time—live in this world, earn a livelihood and all the rest of that? Not "after I have unconditioned myself I will live in the world", but in the very act of freeing, not in the movement of freeing which involves time, but in the very act of freeing live in this world? That is, my education, my culture, my civilization, hasn't given me intelligence. I mean by 'intelligence' sensitivity, the highest form of sensitivity, it is impersonal, it is not your intelligence or my intelligence, or the racial intelligence, or the cultural intelligence. Intelligence has nothing to do with country, with culture, with religion, with persons; it is intelligence. Culture hasn't given me that. But in examining, in watching, in being aware of this conditioning, there is sensitivity to the movement of thought, of time and all that. Out of that highest sensitivity comes intelligence. Now that intelligence will operate when I am living in this world, totally transformed from the world. Are you meeting me? The mind has got a totally new instrument, which is not the result of time. I wonder if you are following all this? That is, sir, freedom is not from something. Freedom is not freedom from conditioning. Freedom is to see the conditioning, to be aware of the conditioning without the movement of thought, and out of that attention, awareness, comes freedom.

Meeting Life, pp. 170-76
Saanen, Switzerland, July 19, 1973

Surely the only true revolution is the freeing of the mind from its own conditioning

So can we really consider this—not as a collective group experiencing something, which is comparatively easy, but as individuals—can we really inquire and find out for ourselves to what degree and depth we are conditioned? And can we not be aware of that conditioning without any reaction to it, without condemning it, without trying to alter it, without substituting a new conditioning for the old, but be aware so easily and deeply that the very process of conditioning—which is after all, the desire to be secure, the desire to have permanency—is burned away at the root? Can we discover that for ourselves—not because someone else has talked about it—and be aware of it directly, so that the very root, the very desire to be secure, to have permanency, is burned away? It is this desire to have permanency, either in the future or in the past, to hold on to the accumulation of experience, that gives one the sense of security—and cannot that be burned away? Because it is that which creates conditioning. This desire, which most of us have, to know and in that very knowing to find security, to have experience which gives us strength—can we wipe away all that?— not by volition, but burn it all away in awareness,—so that the mind is free from all its desires and that which is eternal can come into being.

I think that is the only revolution—not the communist or any other form of revolution. They do not solve our problems; on the contrary, they increase them, they multiply our sorrows,—which again is very obvious. Surely the only true revolution is the freeing of the mind from its own conditioning, and therefore from society— not the mere reformation of society. The man who reforms society is still caught in society; but the man who is free of society, being free from conditioning he will act in his own way, which will act again upon society. So our problem is not reformation, how to improve society, how to have a better welfare state, whether communist or socialist or what you will. It is not an economic or political revolution, or peace through terror. For a serious man these are not the problems. His real problem is to find out whether the mind can be totally free from all conditioning, and thereby perhaps discover in that extraordinary silence, that which is beyond all measurement.

Collected Works, vol. IX, p. 36
London, June 17, 1955

Real revolution is inward

Real revolution is inward, and it comes into being without the mind seeking it. What the mind seeks and finds, however reasonable, however rational and intelligent, is never the final answer. For the mind is put together, and what it creates is also put together; therefore, it can be undone. But the revolution of which I am speaking is the truly religious life, stripped of all the absurdities of organized religions throughout the world. It has nothing to do with priests, with symbols, with churches.

Collected Works, vol. X, p. 63
Brussels, Belgium, June 25, 1956

You cannot cooperate if you are not alone

So a religious mind is a mind that is completely alone. Aloneness is not isolation; it is the actual state of cooperation. You cannot cooperate if you are not alone. Generally you cooperate only when there is a reward or punishment, when you are getting something, when you want to do something together under an authority, under the umbrella of ideas. When you are working for a utopia or an ideal, you are really not cooperating; the idea attracts you, you are absorbed by the idea; and when you disagree with the idea, you break away. That is what is happening with all the communities. In this utopia, ideal society, state, everybody is against another! The communist world is like that too; though they started out to have an idealistic, utopian world, the competition there is more brutal, more ruthless; and they are all trying to cooperate with the state—communes, collective farms; forcing people to cooperate; therefore, inwardly battling, destroying, watching for ways and means where you can go against all this. That is not cooperation.

Cooperation comes only when you are alone, where there is this sense of complete aloneness, which is the outcome, a natural outcome, of a mind that has no escapes, no fear, no authority, and has understood this whole problem of energy. Then it is in a state of cooperation. And, therefore, being in a state of cooperation, it also knows when not to cooperate.

Collected Works, vol. XIV, pp. 117-8
Madras, February 2, 1964

"When once the mind is free, then what is its responsibility?"

As long as the mind is caught in the stream of memory, pleasant or unpleasant; as long as it is held in the chain of cause-effect; as long as it is using the present as a passage from the past to the future, it can never be free. Freedom is then merely an idea, not an actuality. The truth of this must be seen, and then your question will have quite a different significance.

"If I see the truth of it, will there be freedom?"

Speculation is vain. The truth must be seen, the actual fact that there's no freedom as long as the mind is a prisoner of the past must be *experienced.*

"Has a man who is free in this ultimate sense any relationship to the stream of causation and time? If not, then what is the good of this freedom? What value or significance has such a man in this world of joy and pain?"

It's strange how we nearly always think in terms of utility. Are you not asking this question from the boat adrift on the stream of time? And from there you want to know what significance a free man has for the people in the boat. probably none at all. Most people are not interested in freedom; and when they meet a man who is free, they either make of him a deity and place him in a shrine, or they put him away in stone or in words—which is to destroy him. But surely your concern is not with such a man. Your concern is with freeing the mind of the past—the mind that is you.

"When once the mind is free, then what is its responsibility?"

The word 'responsibility' is not applicable to such a mind. Its very existence has an explosive action on time, on the past. It is this explosive action that is of the highest importance. The man who remains in the boat and asks for help wants it in the pattern of the past, in the field of recognition, and to this the free mind has no reply; but that explosive freedom acts on the bondage of time.

Commentaries On Living: Series III, 298-9

IX. The Intelligence Which Brings Order and Peace

Consider what is happening on this earth where man has brought about such chaos, where wars and other terrible things are going on. This is neither a pessimistic nor an optimistic point of view; it is just looking at the facts as they are. Apparently it is not possible to have peace on this earth or to live with friendship and affection for each other in our lives. To live at peace with oneself and with the world, one needs to have great intelligence. It is not just to have the concept of peace and strive to live a peaceful life—which can merely become a rather vegetating life—but to enquire whether it is possible to live in this world, where there is such disorder, such unrighteousness—if we can use that old fashioned word—with a certain quality of mind and heart that are at peace within themselves. Not a life everlastingly striving, in conflict, in competition, in imitation and conformity; not a satisfied or a fulfilled life; not a life that has achieved some result, some fame, some notoriety, or some wealth; but a life that has a quality of peace. We ought to go into it together to find out if it is at all possible to have peace—not just peace of mind which is merely a small part—to have this peculiar quality of undisturbed though tremendously alive tranquillity, with a sense of dignity and without any sense of vulgarity. Can one live such a life?

Has one ever asked such a question, surrounded as one is by total disorder? One must be very clear about that fact; that there is total disorder outwardly—every morning one reads in a newspaper of something terrible, of aircraft that can travel at astonishing speed from one corner of the earth to the other without having to refuel, carrying a great weight of bombs and gases that can destroy man in a few seconds. If one observes all this and realizes what man has come to, one may feel that in asking this question one has asked the impossible and say that it is not at all possible to live in this world inwardly undisturbed, having no problems, living a life utterly unself-centred. Talking about this, using words, has very little meaning unless one finds, or comes upon, through communicating with each other, a state that is utterly still. That requires intelligence, not phantasy, not some peculiar day-dreaming called meditation, not some form of self-hypnosis, but intelligence.

What is intelligence? It is to perceive that which is illusory, that which is false, not actual, and to discard it; not merely to assert that it is false and continue in the same way, but to discard it completely. That is part of intelligence. To see, for example, that nationalism, with all its patriotism, isolation, narrowness, is destructive, that it is a poison in the world. And seeing the truth of it is to discard that which is false. That is intelligence. But to keep on with it, acknowledging it as stupid, is essentially part of stupidity and disorder—it creates more disorder. Intelligence is not the clever pursuit of argument, of opposing contradictory opinions—as though through opinions, truth can be found, which is impossible but it is to realize that the activity of thought, with all its capacities, with all its subtleties, with its extraordinary ceaseless activity, is not intelligence.

Intelligence is beyond thought.

To live peacefully one has to examine disorder. Why do we human beings, who are supposed to be extraordinarily evolved, extraordinarily capable in certain directions, why do we live with and tolerate such disorder in our daily lives? If one can discover the root of this disorder, its cause and observe it carefully, then in the very observation of that which is the cause is the awakening of intelligence. Observation of disorder, not the striving to bring about order. A confused disorderly mind, a state of mind which is contradictory, yet striving to bring about order, will still be disorder. One is confused, uncertain, going from one thing to another, burdened with many problems: from such a way of living, one wants order. Then what appears to be order is born out of one's confusion and therefore it is still confused.

When this is clear, what then is the cause of disorder? It has many causes: the desire to fulfil, the anxiety of not fulfilling, the contradictory life one lives, saying one thing, doing something totally different, trying to suppress one thing and to achieve something else. These are all contradictions in oneself. One can find many causes, the pursuit of causes is endless. Whereas one could ask oneself and find out if there is one root cause. Obviously there must be. The root cause is the 'self', the 'me', the 'ego', the personality put together by thought, by memory, by various experiences, by certain words, certain qualities which produce the feeling of separateness and isolation; that is the root cause of disorder. However much the self tries not to be the self it is still the effort of the self. The self may identify with the nation, but that very identification with the greater is still glorified self. Each one of us does that in different ways. The self is put together by thought; that is the root cause of this total disorder in which we live. When one observes what causes disorder—and one has become so accustomed to disorder and has always lived in such disorder, that one accepts it as natural—one begins to question it and go into it and see what is the root of it. One observes it, not doing anything about it, then that very observation begins to dissolve the centre which is the cause of disorder.

Intelligence is the perception of that which is true; it puts totally aside that which is false; it sees the truth in the false and realizes that none of the activities of thought is intelligence. It sees that thought itself is the outcome of knowledge which is the result of experience as memory and that the response of memory is thought. Knowledge is always limited—that is obvious—there is no perfect knowledge. Hence thought, with all its activity and with all its knowledge, is not intelligence. So one asks: what place has thought in life considering that all our activity is based on thought? Whatever we do is based on thought. All relationships are based on thought. All inventions, all technological achievement, all commerce, all the arts, are the activity of thought. The gods we have created, the rituals, are the product of thought. So what place have knowledge and thought in relation to the degeneration of man?

Man has accumulated immense knowledge, in the world of science, psychology, biology, mathematics and so on. And we think that through knowledge we will ascend, we will liberate ourselves, we will transform ourselves. Now, we are questioning the place of knowledge in life. Has knowledge transformed us, made us good?—again, an old fashioned word. Has it given us integrity? Is it part of justice? Has it given us freedom? It has given us freedom in the sense that we can travel, communicate from one country to another. We have better systems of learning, as well as the computer and the atom bomb. These are all the result of vast accumulated knowledge. Again we ask: has this knowledge given us freedom, a life that is just, a life that is essentially good?

Freedom, justice and goodness; those three qualities formed one of the problems of ancient civilizations, who struggled to find a way to live a life that was just. The word 'just' means to have righteousness, to act benevolently, with generosity, not to deal with hatred or antagonism. To lead a just, a right kind of life, means to lead a life not according to a pattern, not according to some fanciful ideals, projected by thought; it means to lead a life that has great affection, that is true, accurate. And in this world there is no justice; one is clever, another is not; one has power, another has not; one can travel all over the world and meet prominent people; another lives in a little town, in a small room, working day after day. Where is there justice there? Is justice to be found in external activities? One may become the prime minister, the president, the head of a big intercontinental corporation, another may be for ever a clerk, way down below. So, do we seek justice externally, trying to bring about an egalitarian state—all over the world that is being tried, thinking that it will bring about justice—or, is justice to be found away from all that?

Justice implies a certain integrity, to be whole, integral, not broken up, not fragmented. That can only take place when there is no comparison. But we are always comparing—better cars, better houses, better position, greater power and so on. Comparison is measurement. Where there is measurement there cannot be justice. And where there is imitation and conformity, there cannot be justice. Following somebody, listening to these words, we do not see the beauty, the quality, the depth of these things; we may superficially agree but we walk away from them. But the words, the comprehension of the depth of them must leave a mark, a seed; for justice must be there, in us.

Talking to a fairly well known psychologist the speaker used the word goodness. He was horrified! He said: 'That is an old-fashioned word, we do not use it now.' But one likes that good word. So what is goodness? It is not the opposite of that which is bad. If it is the opposite of that which is bad then goodness has its roots in that opposite. So goodness is not related to the other, that which we consider bad. It is totally divorced from the other. One must look at it as it is, not as a reaction to the opposite. Goodness means a way of life which is righteous, not in terms of religion, or morality or an ethical concept of righteousness, but in terms of one who sees that which is true and that which is false, and sustains that quality of sensitivity that sees it immediately and acts.

The word 'freedom' has very complex implications. When there is freedom there is justice, there is goodness. Freedom is considered to be the capacity to choose. One thinks one is free because one can choose to go abroad, one can choose one's work, choose what one wants to do. But where there is choice, is there freedom? Who chooses? And why does one have to choose? When there is freedom, psychologically, when one is very clear in one's capacity to think subjectively, impersonally, very precisely, not sentimentally, there is no need for choice. When there is no confusion then there is no choice.

So what is freedom? Freedom is not the opposite of conditioning; if it were, it would merely be a kind of escape. Freedom is not an escape from anything. A brain that has been conditioned by knowledge is always limited, is always living within the field of ignorance, is always living with the machinery of thought so that there can be no freedom. We all live with various kinds of fear—fear of tomorrow, fear of things that have happened in many yesterdays. If we seek freedom from that fear, then freedom has a cause and is not freedom. If we think in terms of causation and freedom, then that freedom is not freedom at all. Freedom implies not just a certain aspect of one's life but freedom right through; and that freedom has no cause.

Now, with all this having been stated let us look at the cause of sorrow and enquire whether that cause can ever end. All have suffered in one way or another, through deaths, through lack of love, or, having loved another, receiving no return. Sorrow has many, many faces. Man from the ancient of times, has always tried to escape from sorrow, and still, after millennia, we live with sorrow. Mankind has shed untold tears. There have been wars which have brought such agonies to human beings, such great anxiety and apparently they have not been able to be free from that sorrow. This is not a rhetorical question, but, is it possible for a human brain, human mind, human being, to be totally free from the anxiety of sorrow and all the human travail with regard to it?

Let us together walk along the same path to find out if we can, in our daily life, put an end to this terrible burden which man has carried from time immemorial. Is it possible to come upon the ending of sorrow? How do you approach such a question? What is your reaction to that question? What is the state, the quality of your mind, when a question of that kind is put to you? My son is dead, my husband is gone, I have friends who have betrayed me; I have followed in great faith, an ideal and it has been fruitless after twenty years. Sorrow has such great beauty and such pain in it. How does one react to that question? Does one say, 'I don't want even to look at it. I have suffered, it is the lot of man, I rationalize it and accept it and go on.' That is one way of dealing with it. But one has not solved the problem. Or one transmits that sorrow to a symbol and worships that symbol, as is done in Christianity; or as the ancient Hindus have done, it is one's lot, one's karma. Or in the modern world one says one's parents are responsible for it, or society, or it is the kind of genetically inherited genes that have caused one's suffering, and so on. There have been a thousand explanations. But explanations have not resolved the ache and the pain of sorrow. So, how do you approach this question? Do you want to look at it face to face, or casually, or with trepidation? How do you approach, come near, very near, such a problem? Is sorrow different from the observer who says, 'I am in sorrow'. When he says, 'I am in sorrow', he has separated himself from that feeling, so he has not approached it at all. He has not touched it. Can you cease to avoid it, not transmute it, not escape from it, but come with greatest closeness to it? Which means, you are sorrow. Is that so?

You may have invented an ideal of freedom from sorrow. That invention has postponed, separated you further from sorrow; but the fact is, you are sorrow. Do you realize what that means? It is not that somebody has caused you sorrow, not that your son is dead therefore you shed tears. You may shed tears for your son, for your wife, but that is an outward expression of pain or sorrow. That sorrow is the result of your dependence on that person, your attachment, your clinging, your feeling that you are lost without him. So, as usual, you try to act upon the symptom, you never go to the very root of this great problem, which is sorrow. We are not talking about the outward effects of sorrow—if you are concerned with the effects of sorrow you can take a drug and pacify yourself. We are trying together to find for ourselves, not be told and then accept, but actually find for ourselves the root of sorrow. Is it time that causes pain—the time that thought has invented in the psychological realm? You understand my question?

One has had a son, a brother, a wife, father. They are gone. They can never return. They are wiped away from the face of the earth. Of course, one can invent a belief that they are living on other planes. But one has lost them; there is a photograph on the piano or the mantelpiece. One's remembrance of them is in psychological time. How one had loved them, how they loved me; what help they were; they helped to cover up one's loneliness. The remembrance of them is a movement of time. They were there yesterday and gone today. That is, a record has been formed in the brain. That remembrance is a recording on the tape of the brain; and that tape is playing all the time. How one walked with them in the woods, one's sexual remembrances, their companionship, the comfort one derived from them. All that is gone and the tape is playing on. This tape is memory and memory is time. If you are interested, go into it very deeply. One has lived with one's brother or son, one has had happy days with them, enjoyed many things together, but they are gone. And the memory of them remains. It is that memory that is causing pain. It is that memory for which one is shedding tears in one's loneliness. Now, is it possible not to record? This is a very serious question. One enjoyed the sunrise yesterday morning, it was so clear, so beautiful among the trees casting a golden light on the lawn with long shadows. It was a pleasant lovely morning and it has been recorded. Now the repetition begins. One has recorded that which happened, which caused one delight and later that record—like a gramophone or tape recorder is repeated. That is the essence of psychological time. But is it possible not to record at all? The sunrise of today, look at it, give one's whole attention to it, the moment of golden light on the lawn with the long shadows, and not record it, so that no memory of it remains, it is gone. Look at it with one's whole attention and not record; the very attention of looking negates any act of recording.

So, is time the root of sorrow? Is thought the root of sorrow? Of course. So memories and time are the centre of one's life, one lives on them and when something happens which is drastically painful, one returns to those memories and one sheds tears. One wishes that he or she whom one has lost had been here to enjoy that sun when one was looking at it. It is the same with all one's sexual memories, building a picture, thinking about it. All that is memory, thought and time. If one asks: how is it possible for psychological time and thought to stop? it is a wrong question. When one realizes the truth of this—not the truth of another but your own observation of that truth, your own clarity of perception —will that not end sorrow?

Is it possible to give such tremendous attention that one has a life without psychological recording? It is only where there is inattention that there is recording. One is used to one's brother, son or wife; one knows what they will say; they have said the same thing so often. One knows them. When one say 'I know them' one is inattentive. When one says, 'I know my wife', obviously one does not really know her because you cannot possibly *know* a living thing. It is only a dead thing, the dead memory, that one knows.

When one is aware of this with great attention, sorrow has a totally different meaning. There is nothing to learn from sorrow. There is only the ending of sorrow. And when there is an ending of sorrow then there is love. How can one love another—love, have the quality of that love when one's whole life is based on memories; on that picture which one has hung over the mantelpiece or placed on the piano; how can one love when one is caught in a vast structure of memories? The ending of sorrow is the beginning of love.

The Flame of Attention, pp. 102-112
Brockwood Park, England, September 4, 1982

Bibliography

of

books by J. Krishnamurti used in this collection

A Wholly Different Way of Living: Krishnamurti in Dialogue with Allan W. Anderson, London: Gollancz, 1991

The Collected Works of J. Krishnamurti, volumes I-XVII, Dubuque, Iowa: Kendall/Hunt, 1991-2

Commentaries on Living, Third Series, Wheaton: The Theosophical Publishing House, 1988

Education and the Significance of Life, San Francisco: Harper & Row, 1981

The Flame of Attention, San Francisco: Harper & Row, 1984

The First and Last Freedom, San Francisco: Harper & Row, 1975

Meeting Life, San Francisco: Harper San Francisco, 1991

Mind Without Measure, Madras: Krishnamurti Foundation India, 1990

Questions and Answers, Wassenaar: Mirananda, 1982

Talks in Europe 1968, Wassenaar: Servire, 1969

The Wholeness of Life, San Francisco: Harper & Row, 1981